To: Frances

With Love on your 83rd Birthday

Ruth & John xxx

C000125188

C000125188

Memories
of
Accrington

Part of the
Memories
series

Memories

of

Accrington

Edited by John C Goddard

The Publishers would like to thank the following companies for supporting the production of this book

Main Sponsor

Fraser Eagle Limited

The Arndale Centre

Hoyle & Dean Limited

North Lancs Training Group

Simon Jersey Limited

Thompson & Partners

Wolstenholme Funeral Service

First published in Great Britain by True North Books Limited
Units 3 - 5 Heathfield Industrial Park
Elland West Yorkshire
HX5 9AE
Tel. 01422 377977
© Copyright: True North Books Limited 2000

ISBN 1 903204 05 4

Text, design and origination by True North Books Limited
Printed and bound by The Amadeus Press Limited

Memories are made of this

Memories. We all have them: people, places and events, some good and some bad. Our memories of the place where we grew up are usually tucked away in a very special place in our mind. The best are probably connected with our childhood and youth, when we longed to be grown up and paid no attention to adults who told us to enjoy being young, as these were the best years of our lives. We look back now and realise that they were right.

Old photographs bring our memories flooding back - coronations and celebrations; talking pictures, Technicolor and television; the war years, rationing, and the shared hopes and fears which created such a warm community spirit; buying things made of nylon and plastic; fashions which took trouserbottoms and hemlines from drainpipes and mini-skirts to the other extreme; Doris Day, Acker Bilk, Elvis Presley and the Beatles; the jitterbug, the tango and discos; Ford Populars and Minis; decimalisation. Life changed so much over the years.

Some changes were big, some small; some altered our lives in ways we never anticipated. Who in the early days of motoring could have foreseen the motorways and traffic systems of the latter decades of the 20th century? Did any of us realise, when we first saw a computer, what a tremendous impact they would have on our lives? Self-service supermarkets and frozen food made our lives easier - but at the expense of our friendly little corner shops. Nostalgia is always such a mixture of feelings . . . We hope that the collection of pictures in this book will remind you of happy days in bygone eras - and who knows, you might even have been there when one of the photographs was taken!

Contents

Accrington through the years

Blackburn Road taken from the Town Hall roof in 1929

What will Accrington look like at the beginning of the 22nd century? We have no idea, any more than our Victorian ancestors could have foretold, at the turn of the last century, the changes that would come about during the hundred years that lay ahead. Their Accrington was a town which had grown up alongside the thriving cotton industry; there was still plenty of work at the big mills, workers and their families were accommodated in terraced housing, and their daily needs were met by the Co-operative movement, the market and the local traders between them. But change was on its way.

The long struggle to keep King Cotton alive was to grow more desperate, and ultimately many thousands of jobs in the mills were to be lost. Meanwhile, ambitious development plans transformed the town centre. During the 1930s a new road, Broadway, was constructed, and this has taken on a central role in the town of today - though not perhaps exactly the role which the planners of the 1930s had in mind. Contrary to expectations the super cinema which was built at around the same time, and which was seen as crucial to the development of this part of the town, had been demolished again within a few decades.

Motor transport revolutionised town planning, and post-war society put the family car high on its agenda, along with TV and other technological wonders that our ancestors could not have dreamed of. Redevelopment plans in the latter part of the century brought us a redesigned market and a modern shopping centre, where some long-established businesses sit alongside newer names. Two of our great landmarks, the Town Hall and Market Hall, have stood the test of time and have formed the backdrop to many important occasions since Victorian and Edwardian times - coronations, royal visits, civic events and jubilee celebrations of all kinds.

Although we have no more chance of guessing what the coming century will bring than did our forebears, we do have one great advantage over them: we have fascinating photographic records of the town as it used to be and the people who used to live here, and we can look back over these and ponder the changes which have come about. We hope that the collection of photographs in this book will bring back happy memories for older readers of the town where they grew up, while those too young to remember may be able to gain a clearer impression of what life was like for their parents, grandparents and even great grandparents, together with a new insight into some of the factors which have influenced Accrington's development into the fine town we know today.

Accrington Stanley in a photograph dating from September 1960

Around the town centre

The policeman on point duty at the corner of Abbey Street and Blackburn Road is doing a grand job controlling the traffic, but he will not be able to arrest the changes which lie in wait for this part of town. We have no exact date for our photograph, although the network of overhead tram cables confirms it as being post-1907. The buildings visible down Blackburn Road are for the most part still standing, but the area has changed in character since the days when those early motor vehicles with their narrow tyres chattered and rattled over the setts.

With Bradleys on one side and Cash Clothing on the other, there used to be hot competition in the rag trade at this end of Blackburn Road. Bradleys' impressive corner building is for sale at the time of writing, and has a rather forlorn, empty look about it. The Cash Clothing Company had earlier been in premises on the corner of Peel Street, later occupied by Lloyds Bank and Ogden's Jewellers. This building, at the corner of Blackburn Road, was demolished in the 60s after a runaway lorry crashed through the shop window and made the building unsafe.

The buildings down Blackburn Road are for the most part still standing

Above: This is what Peel Street looked like in 1925. We are facing Abbey Street, and the buildings nearest the camera on the left were demolished in the 1960s to make way for the market shops. Motorised and horse-drawn transport are one-all on this shot, though it would not be long before motor cars became the more common sight. Headgear seems to be compulsory for everybody, not only the schoolboy - absolutely everybody is wearing a hat, with the chaps in everything from school cap to flat cap. In the 1920s you didn't feel properly dressed if you went out without a hat. Men would take them off inside public buildings, but women did not; they kept their heads covered until they got back home. Hat etiquette has now largely disappeared, but it used to be considered polite for a gentleman to raise his hat when greeting a lady - just as polite gentlemen always used to hold doors open, give up their seats on buses, and stay on the kerbside of the pavement when walking next to a lady, so that her skirts did not get splashed by passing traffic . . . on the other hand, they weren't in the habit of taking turns at cooking dinner or doing the Hoovering!

Right: King's Hall, situated around the spot where Whalley Road becomes Abbey Street, was not perhaps the most salubrious of Accrington's cinemas, but it was cheap, and it knew how to keep its audiences happy - plenty of action and plenty of excitement, but with the good guys triumphing over the baddies at the end. After all, the Hall, as its square appearance and tall, arched windows suggests, used to be a Methodist Chapel before it was converted to a cinema around 1910, so it was only right and proper that the message spelled out to Accrington's impressionable youth on this particular spot should be that sinners and criminals always get their come-uppance. A glance at the stills posted outside on this occasion confirms that cinema-goers can look forward to another enthralling trip to the Wild West, with plenty of high drama and a soppy bit thrown in for good measure. The smallest of the four advertisement posters is in fact a notice about a Discussion Class at King's Hall. Up until 1915 the cinema was known as the Picturedrome; it then became King's Hall, and introduced talkies in 1931. On 3rd January 1959 it closed down, and stood around doing nothing until the first half of 1962, when it was demolished and replaced by Lloyds Bank.

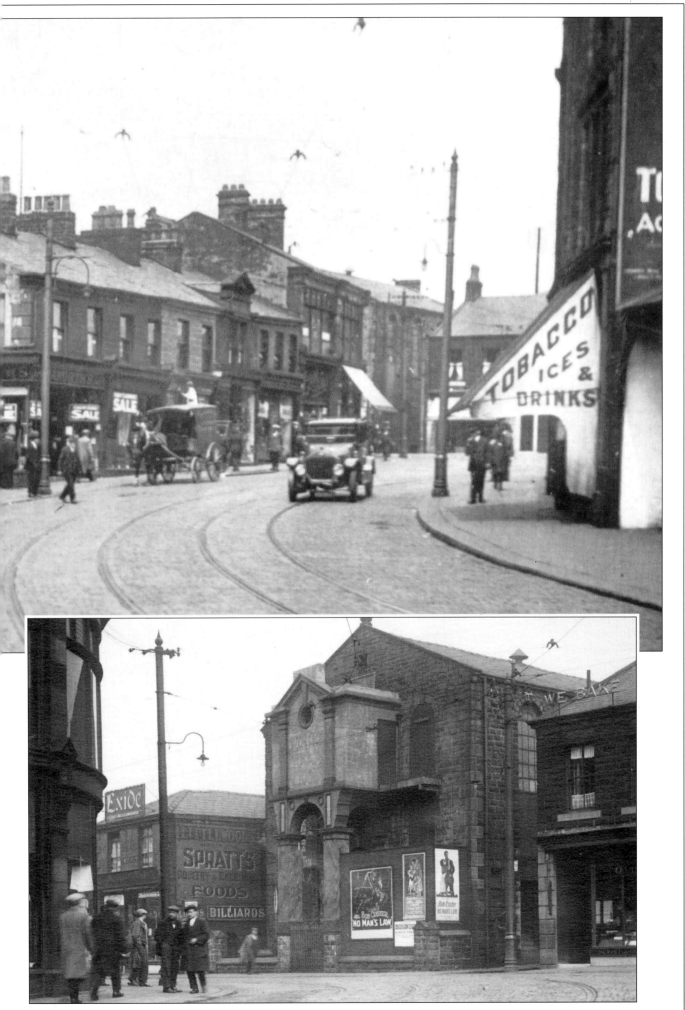

CARS, CHAOS AND COST

Britain saw its very first car in 1894. Twenty years later, in 1914, the world's first traffic lights were installed in front of the House of Commons. Cars were here to stay - but they brought with them their own particular problems.

As traffic levels increased in town centres around the country, various schemes were put in place to control the flow. Some involved the motorist's pocket; in 1947 a Road Tax of £1 per year was imposed.

Road safety also became a major issue, and in 1956 the Ministry of Transport introduced road testing, which at first only affected cars more than ten years old.

To the frustration of the many motorists who were used to free parking, parking meters were introduced to Britain in June, 1958. At the same time, yellow no-waiting lines came into force. A whole new way of life began for the British driver.

Market Hall (seen here with a fair amount of activity in the foreground and a poster which says: Stop! Look who's here! - an enigma which we have failed to solve) was first opened in October 1869 and has stood proudly at the very heart of Accrington ever since. It is a fine building of considerable architectural merit, with elegant classical curves and ornamentation, and together with the Town Hall it gives great dignity to this end of Blackburn Road. On this photograph taken in 1930 the stonework looks relatively clean. By contrast,

pictures of the Market Hall taken during the 50s and early 60s show that it had taken on a distinctly black appearance, which is not altogether surprising in view of pollution statistics for the area; official figures released in 1953 revealed that on average, 17.5 tons of soot were deposited on each square mile of Accrington every month. It has to be admitted that to a lay person this statistic rather defies the imagination - surely with that much soot landing on the town, we would all have been wading around up to our knees in the stuff? Where does it all go? Well, some of it went into coating the buildings, of course; so when the Market Hall's 100th birthday approached in 1969, the town decided that the best anniversary present they could give it was a good clean-up. This was duly done, and the town watched the disappearance of a century of industrial grime with interest.

Left: This amusing sight affords endless opportunities to make scathing remarks about the quality of Accrington's Christmas decorations. The picture was taken for a national newspaper and it doubtless caused a chuckle or two among its southern readers. The poor old Christmas tree had seen better days by the time this photograph had been taken. In fairness, the date on the back of the print is February 1959, so even the smartest tree would have been looking exhausted after two or three months in the heart of the town.

Below: The two ladies approaching the camera on the left look rather as though they might belong to the natty little car parked on the wrong side of the road outside the Market Hall - smartly dressed, bearing themselves very erect and each carrying that essential accessory, the brolly. Apart from this handsome pair, the photographer has captured a good view right along Blackburn Road to the viaduct. In the early part of the 20th century one of the Corporation's pet projects was its scheme to widen Blackburn Road; this was duly carried out, and involved the demolition of a considerable amount of property, including the parade of shops known as Piccadilly which used to stand just opposite the town hall, so that the building line could be taken back. It seems rather ironic, then, that Blackburn Road in front of the Town Hall has in subsequent years been closed to through traffic and narrowed again, with much of the roadway paved over and seats set out on it. The rather functional streetlights seen here have also been replaced by period-style lamps, adding a nice touch to this very pleasant area. And if traffic conditions dictate another change of policy, there won't be any property to knock down - just a few seats to move. At the time of writing it is difficult to imagine why we would want to open the road up again, but then in the first decade of the last century nobody could foresee a time when having a nice wide road to take traffic right through the middle of Accrington would turn into a disadvantage . . .

Left: The railway arch in the distance makes this bird's-eye view of Blackburn Road - taken from the Town Hall roof - instantly recognisable, though not surprisingly some of the details have been modified since 1929. For one thing, the mill chimneys in the background have gone - a minor change in visual terms, perhaps, but one which had an enormous impact on the lives of those who used to depend on the mills for their work. Closer to the camera, the prominent sign of Boots Cash Chemist, as it was in those days, is no longer there - Boots has moved to Cornhill - but apart from that the upper storeys of the buildings in this block have remained pretty much unchanged. Indeed, it is well worth taking a stroll along Blackburn Road and looking up at the fine old masonry on either side of the street, trying to picture these imposing buildings as they must have been in their heyday. There are many attractive decorative and architectural details to admire, including an attractive semi-circular window on the first floor, along past Boots. It is, however, sad to see so many of the properties up and down Blackburn Road standing empty and unloved at the time of acriting. This road used to be the town's main shopping street, and inevitably it faced something of an identity crisis when the commercial centre of the town shifted. We wish it luck for the future.

Above: If you want to sit and contemplate the equivalent view today, there's a conveniently-placed seat just in front of the building which went on to become Age Concern but was originally the Electricity Showroom. However, you won't find too much similarity between the foreground of this picture and the scene in modern times. The light-controlled crossroads has become a roundabout, but the biggest difference is of course that Broadway has been paved; you might see a few vehicles parked down on the right, but you certainly won't see cars and lorries driving the length of it. The Odeon, seen here on the right, has now vanished to make way for redevelopment, along with Cobden Street which used to run alongside it. Now a very elegant block of shops stands here, and adjacent to it up the hill is that nice little corner where you can pause beside the shrubbery and take a breather from all your hectic shopping. Catlow's premises are still there, but have been converted into smaller shop units - and you will certainly never again find grapefruit for 8d (about 3p) each, as advertised here in Catlow's window. However, once we get beyond the hoardings on the left, the view in the middle distance becomes more familiar: the Town Hall shops can be seen to the left, as can the shop units on the right-hand side of Broadway, with Barclays beyond.

The Town Hall was not planned as a Town Hall, and did not actually become known as such until 1878 when Accrington became a Municipal Borough. It was built simply as a memorial to Sir Robert Peel, and was opened as the Peel Institution on Christmas Eve, 1858. Between 1859 and 1878 Accrington Mechanics Institution occupied it, running a library and holding evening classes there until they were able to move into their own building on the corner of St James's Street and Willow Street. The Peel Institution was also used as the Magistrates' Court, and an underground tunnel ran between the Town Hall and the Police Station just round the corner in the original Union Street. The Local Board had in fact purchased the building in 1865, and when the Mechanics moved out, they

moved in. Throughout the 20th century these two grand buildings stood firm amidst constant evolution; the most dramatic changes took place to the side and to the rear, but there are plenty of differences between this photograph and the equivalent view today. The building on the corner of Peel Street was occupied by Lloyds Bank at the time of this photograph. The businesses facing the Town Hall have changed hands, though the premises themselves are little altered, give or take a few chimney pots and a pediment here and there. In Redmans' window is a rather intriguing notice advertising Dried Bilberries - at the risk of doing it an injustice, one imagines that a dried bilberry would be very small, hard and bullet-like, so it is not surprising that they did not catch on.

GETTING AWAY FROM IT ALL

By the end of the 1950s, many town centres which were unfortunate enough to lie along major city routes became bottlenecks, particularly on Bank Holidays. It was clear that something must be done to direct traffic away from town and city streets.

Britain's first stretch of motorway was not, as is popularly believed, the M1. The eight-and-a-quarter miles long Preston Bypass - later part of the M6 - was opened by Prime Minister Harold Macmillan in December 1958.

Vast swathes were cut through the outskirts of towns as ring roads were built to take traffic away from town centres. A network of motorways speeded the average journey, and by the end of the 20th century Britain had 2,015 miles of motorway.

Post-war prosperity meant that more families could aspire to that badge of one-upmanship - a new car. Hot off the production line in 1959 was the Mini - destined to become the 1960s 'car of the decade'.

By the time this photograph was taken, Woolworth's had moved out of the building opposite the Market Hall which they had put up in 1924, and the Co-op had moved in - the notice on their window advises us that they are having a Free Home Purchase Fortnight - so the date is likely to be the late 1960s. We can see that traffic along Blackburn Road is building up, and in the foreground of the picture we have an example of Leslie Hore-Belisha's great contribution to road safety. Traffic accidents first became a matter for Government concern in the period

between the two world wars, when a horrifying 120,000 people were killed on Britain's roads. Measures taken in 1934 included the introduction of the 30 mph speed limit in built-up areas, and the first pedestrian crossings. These were marked out by studs and yellow beacons, but the first beacons were made of glass and made a wonderful target for little boys with stones, so the glass beacons were then replaced by painted aluminium globes. Crossings got their stripes in 1951, and the beacons became plastic and began to wink in 1952. All that remained was to educate people into using them, and a variety of schemes have been tried out over the years to do this - did you join the Tufty Club when you were at school? Nowadays, of course, this section of Blackburn Road is paved over and motor access is restricted, but you still have to look out!

O ld and young alike are taking a moment off to sit and watch the world going about its shopping, on what looks like a bright and sunny day in Accrington - though perhaps unseasonably so, since coats and hats are much in evidence. The tousle-headed youngster seems to think it's warm enough to be ice-cream weather, and is looking hopefully in the direction of the ice-cream stall. Scenes such as this must be exactly what the town planners had hoped for when they decided that this was what the new face of Broadway was going to look like; and no doubt it was also scenes like this which prompted them to carry on with the development and turn Broadway into a traffic-free zone, with plenty of seats so that citizens no longer had to jostle for position and perch on the edges of the flower-beds. The new umbrella market, opened in 1962, was not universally liked to begin with, and took a little getting used to, but the regular market shoppers soon discovered that the market had lost none of its charm in the move; and with the stalls acting as a magnet, the new shopping developments across the road were assured of customers too. The test of a good shopping zone is whether or not it attracts shoppers, and Broadway did.

> *The new umbrella market, opened in 1962, took a little getting used to*

Below: The most obvious casualty since this picture was taken is the clock, and it has to be said that the square, angular structure contrasted rather oddly with the elegant lines of the corner building. Apart from that, little has changed. Peel Street Baptist Church is still there; there is, of course, still a newsagent's present, as every good bus station needs a paper shop, even if it can manage without a clock; and Ogden the Jeweller remains there too. Frank Ogden had only been in possession of the corner spot for a couple of years when this photograph was taken in 1982, although he had occupied the shop round the corner for well over a decade, and had been in business in Blackburn Road since 1924. Before this fine building became a jeweller's it was Lloyds Bank for a long time, while the shop round the side was Curry's before Ogden's moved in. Going back still further, to the very

beginning of the 20th century, Cash Clothing used to occupy this corner, with their name spelled out in huge letters all round the front; that apart, the building looked remarkably similar then.

Bottom: This 60s snapshot must have been taken standing under the canopy at the corner of Redman's shop and Broadway has already taken on an altogether more modern appearance. Wardleworth's has not yet taken up its new position, though, and there are a few changes to be made to the road layout - traffic lights will be installed, and then replaced by a roundabout. The learner driver waiting at the pedestrian crossing may well have had to give a hand-signal before coming to a halt; everyone who learned to drive in that era was taught hand-signals - and didn't you feel stupid, flapping away out of the window to slow down, or

rotating your arm in huge circles to turn left, keenly aware all the while that nobody who had passed their test bothered with them. Passing your test had become practically a rite of passage for the younger generation by the 70s, though a significant proportion of the older drivers on the roads at that time escaped without ever doing so. The driving test was first introduced in 1935, initially on a voluntary basis, and it then became compulsory for everybody who had taken out their first driving licence since 1st April 1934. Initially the Driving Test Organisation set the test fee at 7s 6d (37.5 pence), thinking this would comfortably cover its administration costs; however, so many people sent in their 7/6 that it made a profit of £16,000. So it reduced the fee.

Left: At the time of writing you get the equivalent perspective of the Infant Street and Peel Street junction when you are heading for the loos, though you would be hard put to it to get such a clear view across the road, unobstructed by buses. Even if you could, you would find little similarity with the same spot in the late 1950s. The wooden shack which used to house part of the market has gone; although not in itself a work of art, it did at least protect stallholders and shoppers from the elements rather better than canvas did. After the market moved, Humberstone the jewellers took this spot over and put up a more substantial building, which was later occupied by a variety of shop units. The properties up Infant Street have remained, though Whitewell Dairies - remember their ice-cream? - has long gone. Even in the 50s the advertisement for Worthington would not have been found universally acceptable. Throughout the first half of the 20th century the Temperance movement was very strong in Accrington; it held out for a long time against any form of Sunday entertainment (although as an experiment in March 1944 young people could attend a free Sunday night film show at the Ritz, which included a sermon between the two films) and did its best to help citizens resist the temptation of the demon drink. But inevitably public opinion was eventually swayed by the changing values of society at large, and by March 1959 the Council had voted - though not without some argument - to allow drinks advertisements to appear on their buses.

Above: The Nag's Head - It's A Thwaites House, the sign tells us proudly - was on the corner of Blackburn Road and School Street; this building is still a licensed premises at the time of writing. At the time of our picture in the early 1960s or late 1950s, the parade of shops on the same side as the Nag's Head contained such household names as Timothy Whites and Curtess shoes; most have now changed hands, but not all - Greenwoods the Man's Shop is still there, although the sign is different. Greenwoods' current neighbour Harwoods the jewellers has also been there for several decades; Harwoods had previously occupied another shop further along Blackburn Road, past the railway bridge, and it moved next door to Greenwoods when the old block of railway property under the bridge was pulled down and replaced by the more modern shops which stand there today. Successive generations have left the buildings along the stretch pictured here relatively untouched since the demolition of the Thwaites Arms, which used to stand next to the Town Hall, to make way for the opening of Broadway in the 1930s. Some of these buildings have great character; the two-storey block, for instance, has an interesting castellated roofline, while further along another building bears the tantalising inscription 187-, with the last figure having unfortunately become illegible.

At *leisure*

By 1928 it was compulsory for all children to go to school between the ages of five and fourteen

These likely lads and lasses are Class IIB of the Central Technical School, arranged in an orderly fashion for the photographer. How neat they all look, with not a hair out of place - and the boys in the front row have not only combed their hair, they have also have pulled their socks up and got their ties in the middle - very commendable! In fact these young-sters are particularly fortunate (though they might not see it that way) in being able to enjoy a longer education than their older brothers and sisters. In 1928, which we believe was the year before this photo-graph was taken, it was made compulsory for children to go to school full-time between the ages of five and fourteen. Slowly but surely the school leaving age was creeping up: in 1903 children were required to attend school until the age of 12, and in 1937 the leaving age was raised to 15, although children could leave at 14 in order to start work, if the local educa-tion authority gave its consent. This became a contentious issue, as some said that it was unfair to the poorer families to prevent their children from bringing home a wage at a time when fourteen-year-olds often had a better chance of finding work than adults did, while others argued it would be better all round if families on low incomes claimed benefits instead and let their children stay at school for an extra year.

This page and overleaf: Even if we can't recall the name of the girl or boy we used to sit next to at primary school, the chances are we will remember the characters from our favourite books - Alice, the Famous Five, Thomas the Tank Engine or that loveable rascal Toad out of The Wind in the Willows. The opening of the Young People's Library in June 1938 gave the speakers their cue to reminisce about the books they used to love when they were young. The Mayor, Councillor Ernest Moorhouse, recalled being enthralled by Jules Verne, Henty and the escapades of Deadwood Dick, while Mr Charles Nowell, Chief Librarian

of Manchester and President of the North Western branch of the Library Association, expressed a fondness for Dickens and said that his own children particularly enjoyed Christopher Robin's company. What stories are the children on these photographs listening to, we wonder? Alongside the children's classics that are passed down from one generation to the next, new favourites come and go, and for each generation there are whole worlds full of adventure to choose from: cowboys and pirates, secret agents and gangsters, mysterious masked heroes, fairy princesses, giants, dinosaurs, space aliens and mischievous talking teddy bears.

From previous page: Mr Nowell's advice to the children who were present in his audience was to choose their reading matter carefully; he pointed out that even if you read at the rate of two books a week then you would only get through 5,000 or so in 50 years, and this, by 1938, was a very small proportion of Accrington Library's stock. The library had grown at an impressive rate since its humble beginnings up in the gallery of the Market Hall; the Mechanics Institution had run it for many years, first from the Peel Institution and then from their own premises in St James's Street. In 1908 a new library building, funded by Andrew Carnegie, was opened on the site of Willow House next to the Mechanics Institution. Over the years, bequests from generous benefactors have enabled it to expand its collections and it now caters for every sector of the community. Various extensions and alterations have been made over the years; the young people's library in 1938, a new reference library in 1962 and a Local Studies department in 1990 in part of the former Mechanics Institution.

Above: Not one ripple on the water - wouldn't you just love to dive in and have the pool all to yourself? The year is 1928, and although the exact occasion of this photograph is not recorded we would hazard a guess that the group of swimmers seen here were members of one of Accrington's swimming clubs. There was a keen interest in swimming in Accrington in the early 20th century, although its very first public baths suffered a rather unexpected fate when they somehow contrived to burn down in 1903. The baths seen here are St James's Street swimming baths, which were generally regarded as being very fine: not only did they have plenty of changing cubicles, there was also a proper viewing balcony which made them ideal for swimming competitions and galas. They were to serve the town well for many years, and generations of Accrington school-children had their first swimming lessons here - terrified to begin with and convinced that they would sink like a stone if they let go the rail; then gaining confidence and doing first a breadth, then a length, getting their Third Class certificate, and finally overcoming their fear of the deep end (6' 9"), learning different strokes - and then going on to do their first bellyflop.

Above right: The young lady has put her penny in the slot and is taking advantage of one of the electric hairdryers installed at Accrington baths in 1937. This innovation was of course strictly for the fair sex; chaps, with their short back and sides, had no need of such girlie inventions. However, another innovation at the baths that same year was most definitely of interest to the men as well as the ladies; this was the newly-installed Zotofoam baths which, it was claimed, could help with rheumatism, lumbago, gout and even obesity. All you had to do was spend 20 minutes or so lying up to your neck in warm, soft, cream foam,

letting the tiny air bubbles massage your body, clean your pores, tone your skin, and generally work their wonders on your body - in effect, an early jacuzzi. Just in case readers are left in any doubt as to whether the Zotofoam experience really did improve your health - though whether it improved your figure is another matter - we can assure them that these hi-tec bubble baths found favour in the highest quarters: it is reported that members of the Accrington Stanley team used to use the Zotofoam baths during Cup ties. And who are we to argue with Stanley?

Below: This delightful snapshot was taken in the cloakroom of Lee Royd Nursery School in 1942. The opening of Lee Royd school in April 1936 was something of a triumph for the supporters of nursery education in Accrington. It was the town's very first nursery school, open to children aged from two to five regardless of family background, and was the outcome of a series of visits by education officials to different nurseries around the country. During the course of these visits officials had become convinced of the benefits of nursery schools, in spite of earlier reservations - mainly to do with the cost. Concerns over infant mortality had grown during the 1930s, and not without cause: in 1933 15,000 children aged between one and five had died in the UK. Equally worrying was the fact that many five-year-olds were found to have developed physical defects by the time they started school, which in some cases permanently affected their health. Clearly, the solution was to provide nursery schools where children could grow up in a healthy open-air environment,

with plenty of milk and good, suitable food - on this point, the Chairman expressed the view that children should not eat black pudding - together with exercise, rest periods, and guidance in cleanliness, good habits and good manners. So Lee Royd's two large playrooms and quadrangle faced due south in order to get the sun, and each playroom had its own lavatory accommodation with conveniences, cloakroom and drying room. Outside a sandpit and climbing frame had been installed. In all, the school had cost around £3,600, and before long everybody saw that the experiment was working and agreed that it was money well spent.

Bottom: Early in the 20th century Accrington wanted to build some more schools. In 1906 its proposals for the new Peel Park elementary school were approved, and by the summer of 1910 the building, costing in the region of £17,000, was complete. The opening ceremony was carried out in August of that year, and a very poetic occasion it turned out to be. A special ceremonial gold key was used to unlock the door, and this key seems to have inspired the speakers, who proceeded to wax lyrical about it being the key to the door of knowledge and unknown beauty, and opening 'the entrance to the enchanted garden of enlarged self'. Enchanted garden or not, the school certainly went on to make a tremendous contribution to education in Accrington, while its choir also made quite a name for itself in competitions. Over the next 50 years 8,334 juniors and 4,923 infants passed through Peel Park School - our photograph shows a class of 1950 - and in 1960 the school celebrated its anniversary by giving all the juniors and infants an inscribed pencil, a bag of sweets, ice-cream, and a day's holiday. So there might be a very nice treat or two in store in 2010 for those babies born in the early years of the 21st century who are destined to attend Peel Park School!

Perched on the library step-ladder and looking very cool and poised among the Art books is Miss Barbara Court. Readers may remember the family who lived at the Globe Club where Barbara's parents were the stewards. Barbara joined the staff of Accrington Library around 1960 and was in her early 20s when this photograph was taken for a local paper. And if you think she looks every inch a professional model, you are right. Barbara had already taken the first steps towards a modelling career and it was not very long before she became so successful as a model that she left the library to concentrate on her new interest.

Above: Oakfield House's second career seems to suit it very well. It was originally constructed as the new offices of the Accrington & Church Industrial Co-operative Society. Erected at a cost of £30,000, it was opened on Saturday 17th November 1928 by Mr J Booth JP, the Vice-President of the Society. There was a General Office with a very fine, curved mahogany counter at which members of the Society used to transact their business, while the Society's own private offices were reported to be very pleasant and well-equipped. Co-op employees enjoyed excellent facilities which included a dining room and a special room for them to put their bicycles in. Part of the building was a sales area, and the large shop windows featured displays for the gentlemen's outfitters and for the boot and shoe department. But times and fortunes change, for buildings as well as people; in the mid-1960s the Co-op vacated Oakfield

House and moved into Woolworth's old building, and in 1965 Oakfield House took up bingo. As the photograph shows, it was first known as the New Empire bingo hall, presumably to avoid confusion with the old Empire Picture Palace on Edgar Street. The old Empire cinema had become the Empire Casino Bingo Hall in the early 60s, but when the Bingo moved to Oakfield House the old Empire was refurbished as a cinema again. It was renamed the New Princes, presumably to avoid confusion with both the New Empire and the old Princes, the theatre which had stood next to the old Empire in Edgar Street until it was destroyed by a fire in 1964. Confused? Surely not!

Top: This part of town was transformed beyond recognition during the course of the 20th century. The road layout altered in the 1930s when Broadway was built to link Blackburn Road and Whalley Road. The creation of this new road, which opened during the summer of 1936, was an ambitious project, involving the culverting of the River Hyndburn and the demolition of properties including the Spring Mill buildings and the old Thwaites Arms public house. Accrington's new 'super cinema', opened by Sir Thomas Higham on Monday 12th April 1937, was hailed as a very exciting step in the development of the town. It was originally called the Regal, and with its luxurious auditorium, its exquisite art-deco finish and its second-floor banqueting hall with capacity for 200 people, it put Broadway firmly on the map. However, the outbreak of war curtailed development in this part of town; and ultimately Broadway has turned out very differently from the way the town planners of the 1930s envisaged it, though they would no doubt be pleased to see it playing such a central role in the town. Construction work is still in progress on this photograph, which can be dated by the film showing at the Odeon: Never So Few was released in 1959, and was a star-studded World War II film with Frank Sinatra, Steve McQueen, Charles Bronson and Paul Henreid. The latter may be best remembered for his role in that classic film which is many people's all-time favourite, Casablanca.

Sporting life

Above: A puzzling sight for anyone interested in the fortunes of Accrington Stanley and their Peel Park ground. The mystery deepens with the knowledge that this scene was captured in November 1968 - long after the turnstiles had clicked round for the last time and the final whistle throbbed decisively at the last home game. This evocative action shot was captured by Mr Wally Talbot - a Blackburn photographer on an assignment for a well-known Sunday newspaper. The paper was doing one of those 'looking back' stories, asking what had happened to the famous Accrington Stanley ground since its closure just a few years earlier. The answer was obvious to anyone who could make out the frayed edges of the once proud stand - though the young lads here didn't seem to care. They were reliving the last cup final in Wembley in their own minds, no doubt dreaming of a career with Manchester United, Burnley or Blackburn Rovers.

Above right: "No kidding, it was *this* long" says trainer H. Hubbick to his Accrington Stanley squad in a scene from 1960. Some of the players seem less

than convinced by his angling stories and pretend to be oblivious to the presence of the busy photographer. Starting with the back row we see (left to right) players Jack; Charlie Sneddon; K. Garrity; (middle) Marsden; Brown; Lord; McCreadie; Harrower; Jones and Bennett. Front: Tighe; Jimmy Anders; Kealey; Harry Anders; W. McInnes.

Right: Eleven proud members of the Accrington Stanley squad posed for this press photograph in November 1955. The clean-cut professionals look confident and proud to be wearing the Accrington strip in a photograph that would soon be seen in local and regional papers, not to mention the odd 'national' when there was a space to fill. The picture was taken almost half a century ago, yet some of the names remain familiar to people who follow the game and look back on the days of Accrington Stanley with a real sense of nostalgia. From left to right we see (back row) Messrs. Ash; McCready; McQueen; Harrower; Sneddon and (front row) Cocker; Wright; Stewart; Dick and Scott. The unmistakable shape of the main stand can be seen in the background. Who would have guessed that it would all too soon fall into dilapidation and disrepair?

Below: An Accrington Stanley team picture taken moments before the kickoff. A mixture of emotions is evident on the faces of the players; apprehension, confidence, quiet determination and mild anxiety - you can see them all in their expressions. They faced a game with Reading F.C. on this chilly day in late September 1958. Some of the supporters were taking an interest in the goings-on with the photographer, we can see them leaning over the *Mackeson* advert ('looks good, tastes good and by golly..' etc. etc.) on the touch line. On the skyline a group of mature fans stand mongoose-like in their grey or beige overcoats, topped by flat caps, the uniform of working men on a weekend trip out. We can't see their collars and ties of course, but we *know* they would have been wearing them.

Left: It was a case of 'all hands on deck' in January 1961 when a couple of inches of snow threatened the viability of a Cup match against Preston. We can only imagine how some modern-day professional footballers would react to a request to clear snow from the pitch! These young men obviously rose to the occasion in characteristic good humour, even sparing five minutes to allow Blackburn press photographer Wally Talbot to record the fun in this delightful photograph. For the record, the players concerned were (from left to right) George Hudson; Jack Swindells; Mike Fergusson and, pushing the barrow, Jimmy Harrower.

Below: Accrington Stanley in action, in a magnificent photograph worthy of any Roy of the Rovers epic. It was September 1960, and the home supporters at Peel Park were urging their team forward as bewildered Barrow defenders looked on helplessly. This is a heart warming scene for lovers of local football, but there is a wealth of nostalgia contained in the scene for other readers too. The adverts around the terraces remind us of many local firms as well as some which are not so local yet remain fondly remembered. The clock on the hoarding for *Whitewell Milk* reads 4.25pm, indicating that the match was approaching its conclusion. The most prominent advert is for *Massey's Burnley Ales,* seen on the highly distinctive roof of the main stand on the right and towering over the team benches and dug outs from where encouraging instructions would be directed at the players.

A QUESTION OF SPORT

Manchester United FC were left reeling when an air crash claimed the lives of seven of the 'Busby Babes' and left Matt Busby in a critical condition on 6th February 1958. The plane carrying the team crashed on takeoff from Munich.

The year 1964 saw American boxer Cassius Clay - later Muhammad Ali - (I float like a butterfly, sting like a bee') - beat Sonny Liston to become world champion. In later life he developed Parkinson's disease, but saw himself voted Sportsman of the Century as the new Millennium began.

Wembley Stadium saw scenes of jubilation when on 30th July 1966 England beat West Germany 4-2 in the World Cup. It was Geoff Hurst's two dramatic goals scored in extra time that secured the victory and lifted the cup for England - at last.

The four-minute mile that had remained the record since 1945 was smashed on 6th May 1954 by Oxford University student Roger Bannister. He accomplished the seemingly impossible in three minutes 59.4 seconds, collapsing at the end of his last amazing lap.

Main picture: The teams seen in action here are Accrington Stanley and Plymouth Argyle; we have, however, discovered a conflict of opinion on the date of the photograph, having been variously advised that it was taken in 1955 and 1959. No doubt readers who are able to give positive identification one way or the other will let us know - and they might also be able to name the airborne player on the left who has managed such an impressively high leap in his attempt to head the ball! If the latter date is correct, then the match, played at home on 25th April 1959 before a gate of 3,109, was on its way to becoming a one all draw. Terry Tighe scored for Accrington Stanley, and was to leave the team at the end of the season to transfer to Crewe Alexander. Stanley finished the season 19th in Division Three. However, if we are looking at a 1955 snapshot then the story is somewhat different; 1955 was a great year for Accrington Stanley, and is generally considered to have been the best ever season in the history of that Club. The first team was in the running for promotion but just missed out and had to settle instead for being gallant runners up. The luck of the reserve team held

however, and they won the Lancashire Combination championship and the Combination Cup. The team's success brought its supporters out in force, and that year record gates of over 25,000 spectators in a League game were recorded.

Inset: Here we see Accrington Stanley in action at a time when the club was attracting public interest more on account of the football it played than because of its rocky finances. The origins of the football club can be traced back to the 19th century, although perhaps the most significant dates are 1907 when Accrington Stanley Football Club first became a company, and 1921 when it became a public limited company. Already in 1928 the time was approaching when Accrington Corporation, alerted to Stanley's financial plight, would have to consider starting a fund to save the Club, and

this fund was duly set up during the 1930s. Stanley then struggled on from one financial crisis to the next, and finally on 2nd December 1963 Accrington Stanley (1921) Limited was officially wound up, having been compelled to withdraw from the Football League the previous year. In those days the membership of the Football League was practically set in stone and remained the same from one decade to the next, so this unusual development aroused considerable interest nationally. Overnight the name of Accrington Stanley became known even to people who did not follow football and who knew nothing whatsoever about the Stanley apart from the single fact that they used to be in the league but no longer were. Genuine supporters mourned the loss of their team, and at the time it seemed as though this was the end; however, we now know different.

A driving force in Accrington for over 80 years!

Fraser Eagle Limited has been providing a road transport service from Accrington for over 80 years. Indeed, the business first came into existence in the year 1919. It was in this year that two local men, Harold Williams and Ward Knowles, made the decision to set up in business together. Previously, they had both been working in the passenger/ light haulage business and it was this invaluable experience that enabled them to set up their own coach company.

The two men pooled their resources together and in 1919 managed to buy their first coach, a Crossley. Indeed, it was the purchase of this coach that officially marked the foundation of the new company. The next task on the agenda was that of coming up with a suitable name for the business. This task proved to be more difficult but, was eventually completed out of hours, during a work outing to the local pub! No doubt it was the relaxed atmosphere that, at last, provided the men with the inspiration for a name. One of them made the

suggestion that the new company should be named after his wife's maiden name, Fraser. This was agreed upon and the company was established as Fraser Motors (Accrington) Limited.

Fraser Motors (Accrington) Limited began trading from premises located in the town at 17 Water Street. The premises were actually situated at Harold Williams' home which, apart from his house, also contained a small yard and garage. At first, parts of the premises were rented out for storage purposes to, amongst others, a local joiner.

The business was soon up and running. In these early days, the company did not employ anyone but remained a wholly family run affair. Indeed, the sight of Harold driving the new Crossley coach to wherever it was needed, became a familiar one throughout the town and

Fraser Motors promptly built up a reputation as the coach company that took Accrington Stanley fans to football matches all over the country!

The business began to flourish and it was not long before Harold Williams found himself in a position to be able to buy Ward Knowles' share of the company. Ward had another business venture in mind and was, in fact, keen to sell. As a result, the exchange went through smoothly and Harold Williams became the sole owner of Fraser Motors. Ward, on the other hand, set up his own printing company which became a success and his son is still running the business to this day!

Below: *Harold Williams, wearing a white coat, with Accrington Conservative Ladies on a day trip in the late 1920s.*

Indeed, it was not long before Fraser Motors itself became a family business. This came about when Harold's son, Alec, joined the company. After leaving school, Alec had served his apprenticeship as a mechanic with another company. It was not until completing this training that he joined his father's company and worked as a driver. The father and son team worked well together and the business continued to thrive. The success of the business meant that a second coach was able to be purchased and using these vehicles, Fraser Motors were soon reputed to have the fastest coaches and drivers in the area!

This initial era of success for the company was, in fact, a sustained one which, under the Williams family, lasted for over 40 years. However, by the mid 1960s Fraser Motors (Accrington) Limited had started to decline. The company found itself having to sell some of the coaches it had acquired over the years and unfortunately, by the mid 1960s Fraser Motors only owned one coach. The once renowned turquoise and red Fraser colours had become a rare sight on the local roads and the company was conducting less and less business. It was in this climate of declining trade that Alan Dyson and Harry Knowles stepped in to save the day!

Alan Dyson had started his working life as an apprentice working at Mullards for Philips. After successfully completing his apprenticeship he went on to work for Hebden Brothers, a business that dealt in cars. It was whilst working for Hebden Brothers that Alan met

Harry Knowles. Harry, who was no relation to Ward Knowles, owned his own garage in Rossendale and had to make regular visits to Hebden Brothers. Indeed, it was Harry that first found out about the difficulties Harold Williams was experiencing in running Fraser Motors and that, in fact, he was looking to sell his business.

This discovery occurred due to the fact that Harry was a member of the Rossendale Male Voice Choir. The choir was a very successful one and had won many awards and Eisteddfods. As a result, the choir was always travelling to various events around the country to perform. Coincidentally, the coach company that happened to transport the choir to its various destinations was, Fraser Motors, with Harold Williams at the wheel. Harry and Harold struck up an acquaintance and it was on one of these trips that Harold told Harry he wanted to sell his business. On his next trip to Hebden Brothers, Harry mentioned this information to Alan and together they both decided that they would like to buy Fraser Motors from Harold. Harold was only too happy to sell his declining business to the men and in the year 1965 the deal was completed and Alan Dyson and Harry Knowles became the new owners of Fraser Motors (Accrington) Limited. Initially, Alan and Harry rented the company's Water Street premises from Harold and because they were not sure that the business could

Below: *Harry Knowles, next to the coach door, with members of Rossendale Male Voice Choir in the mid 1970s.*

support both of them they also bought a filling station in New Moss in Oswaldtwistle. This business supported both men whilst they built the coach business back up to its former glory.

Indeed, it was not long before Alan and Harry accomplished their goal and Fraser Motors became a successful venture once again. In fact, the men made such a success of the business that only three years after purchasing it, by 1968, it had outgrown its original premises. As a result, the men moved the business from Water Street to new and larger premises in Tanpits Road. Harold Williams on selling the business retired to Paignton. Sadly however, only six months after retiring, he died and thus ended a chapter in the history of Fraser Motors.

The year 1969 opened on a more optimistic note. By then, the business was flourishing to such an extent that Alan and Harry were able to sell the filling station in New Moss in order to concentrate their efforts on Fraser Motors. This exclusive attention paid off and the business continued in its rapid rate of development and success. Indeed, by the early 1970s the men were able to expand the company. This was achieved by acquiring Harry Duckworth's company, Clayton Le Moors Limited. This company was purchased for its licences which could then be put into use by Fraser Motors.

The late 1970s also proved to be important years in the history of the company. In 1977, Ken Savage joined Fraser Motors straight from school. Ken started work as an office boy but by the 1990s he had worked his way up to the position of Managing Director! In the year 1978, Fraser Motors took yet another step towards expansion. It was in this year that a local company, Eagle Coaches, run by Albert Benson, was purchased by Fraser Motors.

This acquisition had far reaching consequences for the company. Firstly, the company name was changed to Fraser Eagle Limited, incorporating the newly acquired company's name. The company coach colours also changed at around this time and became orange and white. Secondly and most importantly however, a condition of the acquisition was that Jack Duckworth came with the business!

Jack Duckworth was somewhat of a local celebrity and character and his nickname, Jonty, was well known throughout the area. Jonty had worked for many years as a Senior Inspector for Accrington Corporation Transport and on his retirement had gone to work for Eagle Coaches on a part time basis. Fraser Eagle Limited was only too happy to accept this condition and agreed to take Jonty on for 12 months. Little did Harry and Alan know then, that Jonty would still be working for them over 20 years later, in fact, right up until his death in September 1999. Nor could they have guessed that it would be Jonty, alongside Alan, that came up with the idea to start running coach tours as part of the business. Indeed, Fraser Eagle's door-to-door coach holidays have become an extremely successful side of the company's operations and today, holidays are run throughout Great Britain and Europe!

By the 1980s, business was booming and the then, white, red orange and beige colours of Fraser Eagle Limited could be seen throughout the country. The year 1985, was another important one for the company. It was in this year that Fraser Eagle Limited became, once again, a family concern. Alan Dyson's son and daughter both came to work for their father's company in this

Top: *Alan Dyson with Harry's wife at Elswick, Fylde, Blackpool.*

year. Andrew Dyson left school aged 16 and came straight into the business to work in the traffic office. Tracey Dyson, on the other hand, had gained some experience working elsewhere before she joined the company in a secretarial role. During the late 1980s the company formed the retail ABTA travel agency 'Travellers Check-in' which proved to be a highly successful local travel agents, and is still going strong at the start of the new millennium.

Whilst the previous two decades had been years of remarkable success for Fraser Eagle Limited, the early 1990s proved to be a little more challenging for the company. In 1992, Fraser Eagle faced its most threatening problem yet. The holiday company they had been working in conjunction with went 'bust' and as a result, Fraser Eagle also plummeted into financial difficulties itself. Thankfully, this problem was overcome when after having the situation explained to them, the company's creditors all made the decision to support Fraser Eagle in its time of need. Just as the company had managed to recover its losses and get back on an even footing, it was faced with the death of Harry Knowles.

On Harry's death in 1983, 50 percent of his shares in the company were left to his son Andrew Knowles. This meant that Andrew, who had worked for the company for many years, now took an interest in the managerial side of the business. This partnership lasted until the mid nineties when he left Fraser Eagle to join Viscount Central in Burnley.

Other changes around this time included a more positive approach to 'image' and the development of the vivid and most attractive coach livery of blue, green and white with red and gold stripes, together with a massive eagle on the rear corners of each vehicle.

The link with Viscount came full circle when Paul Marney, their operations manager, joined Fraser Eagle, ultimately becoming a board member.

During the same period Jonty's son, Maurice Duckworth, joined Fraser Eagle and thankfully, inherited his father's commendable character! Indeed, it

Top: *A Fraser Eagle coach outside a hotel in Accrington in the late 1970s, the driver is John Westwell.* ***Above:*** *One of the current fleet of luxury air-conditioned coaches.*

was Maurice, in 1996, that had the brainwave which became the company's highly successful Rail Replacement Section. Today, this Section acts as a support network for most of the UK's railway companies and when a rail company has problems it uses Fraser Eagle buses to complete its journeys. Fraser Eagle operates a 24 hour manned hotline and can organise the transport of rail passengers by coach anywhere in the UK. Indeed, on one job a total of 300 coaches were used! With the help of a dedicated team and the very latest computer systems, the company now lead the field in this area!

The year 1999, was another extremely important one in the history of Fraser Eagle Limited. It was in this year that the company reached its 80th anniversary. However, this was not the most remarkable

achievement to take place in 1999. This year also saw the setting up of a Board of Directors in order to cope with the company's diverse business interests and increased growth. Alan Dyson became the Chairman of the company. Mike Royds had worked as the company's bank manager for over 15 years and on his retirement, in this year, he became Fraser Eagle's Financial Director. He was joined by: Barry Cole, Projects Director; Steve Collinson, Fleet Engineering Director; Ken Savage, Managing Director; and Directors, Tracey Dyson, Andrew Dyson, Maurice Duckworth and Paul Marney.

Under this dedicated Board of Directors, Fraser Eagle Limited continued to thrive and has grown into a firm with a multi-million pound turnover. Today, the company employs over 70 people and provides road

transport and support services for train operating and other companies nation-wide. Fraser Eagle has certainly come a long way since its foundation in 1919. Indeed, with plans underway to expand the business further to new premises within the Hyndburn area in the future, there is no doubt that Fraser Eagle Limited will remain a driving force within the industry for many years to come.

Left: *Two of Fraser Eagle's coaches waiting to pick up football fans outside Old Trafford.* **Below:** *One of the company's coaches passing through the archway at Whalley Abbey.*

Events & occasions

Both pages: The floodlit splendour of the Town Hall and Market Hall, which turned Blackburn Road into a fairytale setting at night, was just one of the many fine displays which Accrington put on to celebrate the coronation of King George VI. He was to be crowned on 12th May 1937 - the date originally set for the coronation of his elder brother Edward VIII - and Accrington's Coronation Committee was busy making its plans in the January of that year. The buildings, it decided, would be floodlit from 1st March for a period of three months; other proposals included a firework display on the Coppice and a torchlight procession of Boy Scouts up to the top, a Coronation Ball in support of the Victoria Hospital to be held in October, and one day's holiday with pay to all Corporation employees, to be taken on 12th May or, if that was not possible, on another day in lieu.

firing of the salute, for instance, would cost £5, and after some discussion it was agreed that this should not be approved. But in the end of course it was, and at shortly after 10 am on Coronation Day a Royal Salute of 21 guns was fired by the 125th Infantry Brigade. Throughout the day the Coronation Committee had the pleasure of seeing all the events it had planned being enjoyed by the town, in spite of the weather, which unfortunately was windy and on the cold side, with rain constantly threatening . During the afternoon the over 70s had their feast in the Ambulance Drill Hall, and although it rained for a few minutes at around tea time it cleared up in time for the Scouts' torchlit procession up the Coppice to go ahead. And not only was 12th May itself a day to remember, but the revelry continued for a

P rizes were to be offered for the best decorated public buildings and private dwellings, and another prize was to go the schoolchild who wrote the best essay. Various souvenir gifts for the children were suggested - handkerchiefs with a Coronation design for the infants at nursery school, while it was thought that pupils at the Grammar School and the Arts and Crafts School might be given a choice between a penknife and a fountain pen. The old folk would be given tea and tobacco, and a treat would be arranged for them. It would be nice if the church bells were to ring a peal. A salute could be fired from the Coppice . . . Then the question of cost was raised - could the town afford all this? The Committee did its sums and began looking at some of the proposals again - the

long time afterwards. There was still the Coronation Ball to look forward to, and in the meanwhile many organisations arranged their own dances - indeed, these had started as early as April. It was nice to have something to celebrate. For one thing, after the scandal surrounding the abdication of King Edward VIII, everybody was eager to welcome his shy, unassuming and very likeable younger brother to the throne; and for another thing, unemployment had become a fact of life during the 30s and people were having to live with the depressing realisation that the cotton industry would never regain the prosperity which it had enjoyed in the previous century. Those who took an interest in world politics were possibly beginning to find the international news a little worrying, too . . .

The year is 1932, and the scene is set for an important ceremony to take place: the laying of the foundation stone for Accrington's new police station, to be performed by the Home Secretary Sir Herbert Samuel. Judging by the bowed heads and somewhat preoccupied manner of those on stage - who include the Mayor's attendant and Town Hall keeper Mr T G Nelson, the Mayor himself, and Mr Warhurst, Town Clerk - proceedings have not yet got underway; only the Mayor, Councillor Constantine, seems ready to begin. Alderman Waddington, standing in front of the stage, appears to be taking a keen interest in the construction materials, and indeed the brick versus stone

controversy ran on for a long time, as many local people felt it was only right and proper to use Accrington bloods, and objected strongly to the proposed use of Yorkshire facing stone. Yorkshire stone, however, was what the plans stipulated. The plans had been chosen from a dozen entries in a competition which invited architects to design brand new premises for not only the police station and the court, but also the fire station. This ambitious project took around three years to complete and provided welcome employment during these economically depressed years. The opening ceremony took place on 9th May, 1935, and everybody agreed that the buildings were very fine indeed, and a credit to the town.

A Royal tour of Lancashire was planned for late Spring, 1938. Naturally Accrington featured on it, and even though the town was only allocated a 12-minute slot - 11.30 to 11.51am on Tuesday 18th May - it made the most of it! When Tuesday morning arrived, Market Place began to fill, until - as this photograph shows - there was barely a spare inch anywhere. The schoolchildren were assembled, all wearing souvenir buttons with photographs of King George VI and Queen Elizabeth. While final preparations were being carried out up on the stand, amplified gramophone music was played to the crowd; and exactly on schedule the Royal party nosed its way into Market Place. Loud cheers filled the air, 4,000 or more Union Jacks were twirled about excitedly - we are told that the flagsticks had been removed from the children's flags to prevent them poking each others' eyes out in the crush - and with flags and bunting fluttering in the breeze the Royal couple stepped up onto the stand. All went according to plan. Twenty-eight local people were presented to the King and Queen, the minutes simply flew past and all too soon it was time for the Royals to move on, leaving behind them memories of the moment for the people of Accrington to cherish for many years to come. What many people remembered best was Queen Elizabeth's beaming smile, which had earned her the nickname of The Smiling Duchess before the accession, and which ensured that she remained tremendously popular during her daughter's reign, as the Queen Mum.

Below: Accrington's handsome Town Hall - seen here standing next to the Thwaites Arms which was demolished in the 1930s - has flown the flag for many Royal occasions in the course of its existence, and we believe that the Union Jacks and bunting which adorn it on this photograph are there in celebration of the coronation of King George V in 1911. In the days before television, it was left to each town and city around the country to mark occasions of national significance as it saw fit. Although the ceremonies taking place in London on 22nd June 1911 were in everyone's thoughts, nobody outside London would actually see any of it until the photographs appeared in the papers the next day. So Accrington staged its own pageantry: the Mayor and Corporation left the Town Hall at 9.00am and processed in state to St James's Church, where a coronation service was held at 9.15. The procession then went on to Oak Hill Park. Here the bands continued to play throughout the morning, and a programme of Morris dancing had been arranged. As the day wore on festive crowds continued to gather at various spots around the town, and in the afternoon there was hymn singing, more processions, more music and more dancing. At 10pm the enormous Coronation bonfire in Peel Park was lit. Fortunately the weather remained generally fine, and from morning until night the whole town was a place of rejoicing as the people of Accrington joined together in public celebration of the crowning of their new monarch.

Bottom: King George VI and Queen Elizabeth were no strangers to Accrington; they had visited the town in May 1938, and on 8th March 1945 they were back again. Although Germany's official unconditional surrender was still awaited, we knew that we had won the war. Our heroes were starting to return to civilian life from active service; and one of Accrington's numerous war heroes was Squadron Leader Peter Rippon, who was to receive the decoration of the Distinguished Flying Cross from the King on 8th March 1945. Peter Rippon was the son of a director of Howard & Bullough, where he had worked up until joining the RAF, and the investiture was to take place at the firm's premises. Crowds lined the streets to welcome the King and Queen to Accrington, with rows of children standing at the front, all neatly turned out and many of them in uniform, with Guides, Brownies, Scouts, Sea Cadets and ATC among them. The Royal party arrived during the morning; Queen Elizabeth was in pastel blue, and King George VI was wearing the uniform of Air Chief Marshal of the RAF, as befitted the occasion. They were greeted by the Mayor, Councillor G E Slack, before proceeding to tour Howard & Bullough's works. The workers there had been instructed to continue with their jobs as usual, and the King showed great interest in what they were doing, stopping now and then for a chat, before going on to perform the investiture ceremony which was the climax of his visit.

Left: We know who the men are: they are our Fire Brigade, back in the late 1940s or early 1950s - and we even know some of their names: Harry Swindlehurst, Charles Hogan, Jack Smith, George Yeoman, Bill (Slobber) Sutton, Alan Bradshaw and Bill Jeff are among them. However, we are not quite so sure what they are all looking at. Officially, this is a picture of Divisional Fire Officer Crabtree demonstrating the aerial-maroon call-out system, which we are informed was for use in case the alarm bell failed. The amused smiles on the faces of the men could be interpreted either as meaning that they think it is a truly marvellous invention, or they are not convinced by it at all. Without inside information, the contraption appears quite incomprehensible; however, if all else fails then the metal bin should make plenty of racket if you kick it hard enough.

Below: This photograph was taken on 20th June 1940, the year before Accrington Fire Brigade became part of the National Fire Service. Subsequently it became part of the Lancashire County Fire Service. In the early days of the Brigade, the three emergency services tended to share manpower, so firefighting was just part of the men's responsibilities - and in addition to their ambulance duties they apparently also assisted with the street-lighting. However, by 1935 the Fire Brigade had made great progress in terms of premises and equipment; its new premises opened on 9th May 1935, and into them moved a Brigade consisting of 50 firemen and three appliances. The last steam-powered appliance had recently been disposed of. The following year they purchased the immense turntable ladder seen behind then in this picture; it is a Leyland Metz TTL, and the ladder is 100 feet long. This impressive appliance was one of the first of its kind anywhere in the country, and set Accrington Fire Brigade back £3,695.

THE CAUSE THIS DAY IS WORTHY OF YOUR GENEROUS SUPPORT, is the message on the windows of this splendidly-decorated Accrington Corporation tram decked out for Victoria Hospital Fete Day on Saturday 14th August 1926. Opened in 1898, Victoria Hospital's buildings had been extended only once, in 1907, after which it was able to provide accommodation for up to 50 in-patients. The Hospital Extensions Fund had been launched in 1925 to try and raise £40,000 for a nurses' home, new male, female and isolation wards, and additions to the existing facilities. The Mayor's Victoria Hospital Fund was set up to assist, and ran a series of events including American teas, concerts, dances, a cricket match, a dance display at the Hippodrome by juniors, a Flower Day which raised over £200, and finally Fete Day. This featured a procession a mile and a half long, and everybody agreed it was the best procession the town had had for years. The Mayors' Fund had aimed to raise £1,000, and in the end it was able to hand over £5,144 11s 9d; this, added to around £10,000 which the public had donated to the Extensions Fund and monies received from other sources, made a grand total of £39,959 5s 7d by the end of 1927. Work had begun on the Nurses' Home earlier in the year, and no doubt the hospital was relieved to find funds flowing in so quickly; following the completion of the previous extensions in 1907, it had taken them until 1916 to clear the debt.

Below: The severe floods in 1960 caused untold misery to local families. It is difficult to imagine how this brave woman summoned up the strength to smile for the camera, posing pitifully with her teapot for the curious readers of a local newspaper. Yes, people were made of sterner stuff in those days. Consider the disastrous effect the flood waters had on local folk: few had insurance cover to replace damaged possessions. Not that many of them had much, but what they did have was ruined by the stinking, muddy liquid that seeped through the brick and plaster work with the devastating thoroughness of the devil himself. Coal cellars were the first to be swamped of course, making the prospect of lighting

any fire in the house somewhat more than challenging. And children still needed to be fed and clothes to be washed. Day to day activities which were hard at the best of times became enormous tasks and were only achieved with the help of the neighbours and relatives who rallied round in true Lancashire spirit. The mess and upset were to remain long after the newspaper men had lost interest.

Bottom: A remarkable coincidence resulted in this photograph being taken and then used in many national newspapers up and down the country. Past followers of Accrington Stanley might recognise the beaming faces of the lantern-jawed young men in the picture. They are, of course, the *Anders twins* - Harry on the left and brother Jimmy on the right. The scene was captured in a local maternity hospital on February 24th 1959 and the remarkable coincidence was that the wives of the famous twins had given birth to two sets of twins themselves - at chances of many millions to one. Overnight the size of their respective families had doubled - much to the obvious delight of the happy parents shown here.

Above: Posing for the photographer in front of the Girls' High School are the men of the Home Guard, 7180 Accrington Battalion. The year is 1943, and the immaculate turn-out and proud bearing of the men speaks for itself. Although in subsequent years television programmes such as Dad's Army have chosen to make light of life in the Home Guard, they performed excellent work all over Britain in keeping a lookout for invaders, manning anti-aircraft rocket guns, organising balloon barrages and liaising with other units and with regular troops. It is true that the force relied heavily on improvisation in its early days. When Sir Anthony Eden, Secretary of State for War, appealed over the radio at the start of the second world war for men between 17 and 65 to form the Local Defence Volunteers and guard vulnerable points from Nazi attack, volunteers immediately began to come forward. Accrington's LDV was headquartered at the Mechanics Institution, and to begin with they, like volunteers all over Britain, made do with whatever bits of military kit they could get their hands on until proper weapons and uniforms were provided; in many cases the old joke about using broom-handles for bayonets during training was not a joke at all. The bravery and devotion of the Home Guard, as the LDV was renamed, has gone down in history - and it was nice to discover, alongside the original photograph to which we were given access, a page bearing the signatures of many of the men pictured.

Right: Spring Hill School must have had more opening ceremonies than any other school in Accrington. The one seen here is the opening of the Infants' Department on 21st December 1932. The school itself was not new; it had been erected towards the end of the 19th century as a Wesleyan day and Sunday school, as a result of a scheme initiated by Alderman Smith who died before the schools were finished, and the first opening ceremony of the Spring Hill Smith Memorial Schools took place in 1899. The Council then took the school over in 1905, and it became a mixed school. The Infants' Department, which consisted of three classrooms, a playroom/assembly room and cloakroom and lavatory accommodation, was added as part of a £10,000 extension scheme which also provided extensions to the mixed department. At the opening ceremony Councillor Constantine expressed satisfaction that there was now provision for nursery classes, with supervision for two to five-year-olds, but added that this was not the same as a nursery school. Nursery schools were a new idea at that time; Accrington had none and was still undecided as to whether or not it wanted any, with Councillor Constantine himself being in favour. In fact, within four years the first nursery school, Lee Royd, was built, and on 22nd March 1952 another opening ceremony was held at Spring Hill - this time to open the town's second proper nursery school.

MILESTONES ALONG THE WAY

On 29th May 1953
Sir Edmund Hillary and Sherpa Tenzing Norgay conquered Everest, the world's highest mountain, using the most modern equipment of the day. On the summit they left the Union Jack, the flag of Nepal and the United Nations flag.

During the 1950s a *lethal mix of smoke and fog - labelled smog - descended regularly on Britain's town's and cities. In London alone the deaths of over 4,000 people were directly linked to smog in 1952. Three years later the Clean Air Act was passed to address the problem.*

Twenty-eight year old *Ruth Ellis went to the gallows in July 1955 for murdering her former lover, racing driver David Blakely. She was the last of 15 women hanged for murder in Britain during the 20th century. Capital Punishment ended in 1964.*

Decimalisation brought *confusion (and a rise in prices) to Britain in 1971. It was far easier to reckon in tens than in twelves and twenties, but all the same it was to be years before people stopped checking prices by mentally converting them into 'old money'.*

A good cross-section of age groups has been captured on this photograph, taken at a St Patrick's Ball at the Ritz during the 1950s. The Ritz Ballroom and Restaurant was opened on 13th December 1934. That same month the nearby cinema in Church Street, previously known simply as The Picture House, was renamed The Ritz, the reason being that it was the cinema's current owner who had built the ballroom. Irish Balls were soon established as a regular event at the Ritz Ballroom, and generally attracted well over a thousand people. During the war Accrington Town Council was

thrown into some confusion by a proposal to hold jazz dances at the Ritz every Saturday night, as it was torn between feeling it was not quite proper for the town to enjoy itself so much when the nation was at war, and realising that it was important to keep people's spirits up. In the end someone suggested a compromise: the dances could be held once a fortnight. It was of course not until the late 50s that the new American music really caught on in this country and bands began to include rock and roll sequences in amongst the jazz and the traditional waltzes and foxtrots. By the end of the decade some of us were rocking and rolling, and others of us were so shocked by Elvis Presley's obscene gyrating hips that we wanted nothing to do with rock and roll and sat those dances out, returning to the floor when the band struck up something a little more to our taste.

Pages 62 - 67: *Accrington dressed itself up for the coronation of Queen Elizabeth II in more than 2,000 yards of bunting and 100 royal blue flagpoles; at night the Town Hall was illuminated by 1,000 coloured lights, while next door the Market Hall, not to be outdone, was decked out with fairy lights (though here statisticians will be disappointed, as the exact number does not seem to have been recorded) and both buildings featured the grand illuminated letters EIIR. There were more lights throughout the town, including floodlights at the Sunken Gardens on Broadway and St James's Church, and all these were switched on during Coronation Day itself. In addition to the decorations put up by the Council, the shops had their own colourful displays, and householders had joined in the spirit of the occasion too; so all in all Accrington was looking about as festive as a town can look. Everybody had been busy making plans: the official programme of events ran over several days and included everything from processions and dancing to sports and open-air worship.*

FURTHER AFIELD....

Plans to develop the economies of member states into one common market came into being on 1st January 1958, when the EEC was formed. The original members were France, Belgium, Luxembourg, The Netherlands, Italy, and West Germany. Britain became a member in 1973.

Barbed wire and concrete blocks divided East from West when the infamous wall was built across the city of Berlin in 1961. Many escaped to the West at the eleventh hour, taking with them what they could carry. The Berlin Wall divided the city until 1989, when Communist rule collapsed.

The 2nd March 1969 was a landmark in aviation history. The Anglo-French supersonic airliner Concorde took off for the first time from Toulouse in France. Concorde was designed to fly from London to New York in an incredible three hours twenty minutes.

Neil Armstrong made history as the first man to set foot on the moon on 20th July 1969, and the phrase 'One giant leap for mankind' was coined. Twenty-one hours and thirty-seven minutes after their landing, he and 'Buzz' Aldrin took off again, proudly leaving the American flag on the Moon's surface.

From **previous page:** Broadway car park was the place to be on the evening of Coronation Day itself, when dancing to gramophone records took place there from 9pm onwards. Saturday was declared Gala Day. Highlights of the official programme included a Coronation procession and a swimming gala at St James's Street Baths, and, on 31st May, the Combined Churches Procession: twelve Free Churches joined in a Coronation

procession half a mile long, which wended its way to Oak Hill Park. Our photograph shows the huge crowd which gathered in the Park, where an open-air service was held - and what a wonderful and heart-warming picture it is, with so many nicely-dressed little children standing there beside their parents and grandparents. The service began -

of course - with the National Anthem, which was followed by prayers and then hymn singing, with one of the hymns being Rejoice O Land in God Thy Might. The Reverend A McLean spoke in his address about the role of the Royal family and the importance of family life - topics which are as pertinent today as they were then.

From previous page: The Coronation certainly provided an occasion for families to celebrate together, and above all everybody did their utmost to make sure it was a special occasion for the children. Little communities all over the town had been planning their own programme of events, which involved decorating their bit of the street, baking goodies for their street party, making party hats, and buying gifts for the children. All this had to be funded by street collections, which typically raised anywhere between £10 and £30. Older readers who were involved in the organising may recall that

Beetle Drives were a very popular and successful method of raising funds, whereas younger readers will have been interested not in the fund-raising but in eating the good things laid out on the table! But the one thing that set this Coronation apart from those that had preceded it was, of course, television. All over town households who possessed a television set opened their doors to as many people as could squash into their living room, and many people in Accrington, together with millions more all over Britain, watched television for the first time in their lives on June 2nd, 1953.

There are some events which never lose their appeal, and bring-and-buy sales are among them. You just never know what you will find, and there's always the chance that the bargain of a life-time is waiting for you on the next stall. Here we see Accrington Forget-me-Not Club, whose bring-and-buy sale will begin once the meeting is over. The good works of these ladies and gentlemen did a great deal to improve the quality of life for the elderly of the area. Nowadays we can look forward to a long retirement with reasonable confidence, knowing we can rely upon Age Concern, Help the Aged and other such well-established national organisations to make our mature years easier, but around the middle of the 20th century people were only just beginning to give serious thought to the consequences of increased life expectancy. The Forget-me-Not Club was, we believe, one of the first organisations to become actively involved in supporting the area's elderly. As with many charitable organisations, finding suitable premises in which to settle was sometimes a problem. At one stage Accrington Forget-me-Not Club found a home in Eagle Street, which it moved into in 1968. Our picture, however, was taken inside Avenue Parade Methodist Church, later demolished; the Peel Health Centre was built on the site. Sir William Cocker stands at the centre of this Forget-me-Not Club gathering. To his right is Mrs Elizabeth Swift.

did not survive. In financial terms, the cost of the damage was put at around £2million, but no price can ever be put on the human misery and heartache caused by tragedies such as this.

Top: By mid-1945 Accrington had a waiting list for houses a thousand names long, and voices were crying out that it was all the Corporation's fault for not building enough in the years between the wars. So the Corporation was under great pressure to produce dwellings for all these people; what it really needed was a miracle, and numbers 73 and 75 Ribblesdale Avenue, seen on this photograph, were the closest thing to a miracle it could hope for. On 13th August 1945 this pair of experimental houses was opened for public exhibition, having been built, decorated and fully fitted out in less than five weeks. They were concrete. The walls were made in a mould and ready in eight days, and within a fortnight the roofs were on. Inside, the houses were well proportioned with plenty of cupboard space, and they met with a generally favourable reception, particularly from women. So the Corporation was off the hook, and could prepare contracts for scores of Easiform houses. By April of the following year the first ones, in Richmond Road, were ready for occupation; a total of 128 were built on the Fern Gore and Richmond Hill estates, at a cost of less than £1,100 each. Certainly this new, speedy method of construction provided many homes for people who desperately needed them. However, within the decade the Corporation had recognised that there were disadvantages to concrete houses, and had come to the conclusion that on the whole it preferred to build its houses out of bricks and mortar.

Above: From the bits of car that are visible, it would seem that we have here a Ford Anglia and either a Ford Zephyr or a Ford Zodiac, bobbing about above Grange Lane car park like two ducks on a pond. We trust they are unoccupied; during the catastrophic floods of Saturday July 19th, 1964, there were reports of cars being swept along for distances of up to a quarter of a mile. Thunder and heavy rain started early in the morning of the first Saturday of Wakes fortnight, and when the deluge reached its peak just before midday, drains and culverts could no longer cope with the inches of torrential rain which came hammering down in just a few hours; one theory was that they were blocked with debris. In some areas - of which Grange Lane was one - flooding wreaked absolute havoc. The Accrington to Manchester railway line via Bury was blocked near Baxenden, mills and warehouses were damaged, and so many houses were flooded out that a Mayor's Relief Fund was set up to help the numerous families who were left homeless. There were hair-raising tales of narrow escapes from buildings as the flood waters rose, and sadly there were some who were not so lucky and

Both pictures: The announcement that Queen Elizabeth II and the Duke of Edinburgh were to stop off at Accrington on Thursday April 14th, 1955, as part of their Royal tour, created quite a stir; and what was even better was that the visit was scheduled to take place at lunchtime, so that even the workers would be able be join the crowds. Long before the Queen was due to arrive the streets were packed with young and old alike, and every window was full of heads craning to get a good view. It was the first time Queen Elizabeth II had been to Accrington, although her parents had visited the town almost exactly a decade before, in March 1945, and the weather for the young Queen's visit could not have been better - it was a perfectly glorious Spring day. So the assembled crowds were able to enjoy the sunshine as they waited, and a tremendous atmosphere of excitement and eager anticipation built up as 12.30 approached. For many people, it must be said, this event was perhaps the brightest spot in what was otherwise a rather dismal year; 1955 was a year of industrial unrest and strikes over pay, with railwaymen and dockers among the groups regularly in the headlines - when newspaper production was not brought to a halt, that is - and

the cotton industry was still struggling bravely on against all the odds. But none of these troubles are reflected on the faces of the crowd, and when the Royal party arrived outside the Town Hall just five minutes behind schedule, at 12.40, a deafening cheer went up, flags were waved, and the Queen and the Duke of Edinburgh were welcomed to Accrington by a sea of happy faces. The Royal couple were greeted by the Mayor, Councillor Michael Walsh, and ushered inside the Town Hall to sign the Distinguished Visitors' Book and autograph photographs of themselves; but before entering the building, Queen Elizabeth paused for a moment in the doorway, then turned and smiled at the crowd all around her. It was a moment which many of those present would never forget - the moment when our beautiful young Queen stood in our midst, outside the Town Hall, and smiled that wonderfully warm, genuine smile which had already captivated the hearts of the nation, but this time it was just for the people of Accrington. When the Royal visitors emerged from the Town Hall a short while afterwards to continue their journey, travelling via Peel Street, Whalley Road and Burnley Road, they were cheered along their entire route until they were over the Borough boundary.

This is a Mayor's Sunday procession, and we take it that the Union Jacks and bunting along Blackburn Road have been erected in honour of the 1953 Coronation, thus giving us the year of the photograph. Fittingly enough, the year of Queen Elizabeth II's coronation was also the year in which Accrington voted in its first lady mayor. The lady in question was, of course, Mrs Grace Rothwell, who six years earlier had also become the first woman to be elected to Accrington Town Council, on 10th June 1947. It seemed that everything had conspired to make this an altogether unique occasion; not only had Accrington got its first lady mayor in the year our new Queen came to the throne, but the new lady mayor

even had a new robe to wear; it had been decided some while previously that the mayoral garb was due for renewal, and the town had invested in a fine new red robe. The people of the town have turned out to hear the band and watch the procession, which as can be seen stretches right down Blackburn Road, past the Commercial Hotel and almost out of sight. Six years hence, Mrs Rothwell was to notch up another first when on 21st May 1959 the Council voted her the town's first lady Alderman.

AROUND AND ABOUT

Christmas 1957 saw the beginning of what was to become British tradition when the Queen made her very first television Christmas broadcast. Her grandfather King George V was the first monarch to broadcast a Christmas Day message over the radio.

The Beatles' first single 'Love Me Do', produced with Parlophone in 1962, turned the music scene upside down - and Decca were left kicking themselves for rejecting the 'Fab Four'. Three years later the Beatles received MBEs from the Queen.

Loud cheers greeted the jury's verdict when D H Lawrence's banned novel 'Lady Chatterley's Lover' was passed for general readership in 1960. The initial print-run of 200,000 copies detailing the erotic encounters of the lady and her gamekeeper sold out on the first day.

On the move

Below: The bridge over Blackburn Road was a good read, back in 1921. Borough Building Society, established in Burnley in 1874 and now with a local office at 20 Willow Street, has got pride of place, while on either side of the arch, with pleasing symmetry, is an advertisement for pastilles. Robinson's Barley Groats, featured on the left, must surely have been a foretaste of the Barley Water which is still popular today. The rest of the literature on the bridge is devoted to advertising forthcoming events. For those who are in the mood for music, there is a poster listing the bands which are appearing at the Hippodrome; for those of a more serious turn of mind, there is another poster advertising Elijah at the Town Hall; while those who feel like indulging in a little escapism might be more interested in the notices posted by the Empire and the Palace. One of Palace Pictures' offerings is entitled On Your Toes, and this we take to be a production of the play which was a Broadway hit some years later. The storyline is about the rather complicated goings-on backstage at the ballet. A film version was made, but we understand that this was not released until 1939, many years after this photograph was taken. These days, the structure is kept clean and bill posters have to make do with any conveniently-situated empty units.

We are informed that this was the first motor bus to leave Accrington for York, and back, and it is certainly the centre of attention as it prepares to set off. Its departure point was clearly outside the Commercial Hotel - now the Regent - as Market Chambers can be seen in the background; Joseph W Bridge occupied his spot for many years, and next to him on this picture is the piano shop of Ebenezer Coupe and Son, advertising Bechstein and Chappell pianos, two of the best makes on the market in the days when nobody had ever even heard of Yamaha. The year 1903 has been suggested as the date of this photograph. The Habergham is a very elegant, well-finished vehicle, with that wonderful sweeping staircase and the delicate coach stripes around the passenger door and the upper deck. It looks rather as if there is a covering to fasten across the doorway once all the passengers are aboard. We have not been able to discover how long the journey was scheduled to take, and in any case we would prefer not to have to compare The Habergham's performance with a modern bus; if the vehicle's looks are the sole criteria, surely everybody will agree that The Habergham is much prettier!

Buses have long fulfilled a dual role as they rumble around our towns - they transport people from A to B, and they act as mobile advertisement hoardings. The double-decker pictured here in Peel Street in the 1950s is giving its message about Ozone bleach loud and clear. Not everybody thought that this was what the sides of buses were for, however, and one of those did not, and who was not afraid of speaking out on the subject, was Councillor Constantine. It is recorded that on 3rd April 1950 he told a Council meeting exactly what he thought of having 'hideous advertisements' on the Corporation's buses. The Council, perhaps calculating the revenue that would be lost, disagreed with Cllr Constantine on this point. Not that this was anything new; Cllr Constantine will be remembered by many readers as a man with strong views and a forthright, not to say outspoken, manner, a committed Methodist and Temperance worker who gave long and invaluable service to the town. Although the Council chose to disregard his opinion on the matter of bus advertising they did listen to him on many subjects which were, it can safely be said, of infinitely greater long-term significance to the town and its inhabitants.

were not at all sorry when the tram-lines were taken up were the cyclists. Getting your front wheel wedged in a tramline was an ever-present danger, and could be a very unpleasant experience - especially if there happened to be a tram bearing down on you at the time!

Top: Since buses came to Accrington in the late 1920s, we have had all kinds of different models, and regular bus travellers will all have developed their own preferences over the years. The more modern ones like this pictured in 1963 with the automatic doors were usually nice and warm and comfortable, but one-man (or woman) operation caused quite a fuss when it was introduced. The older style double-decker with the open platform and staircase at the back, an example of which can be seen behind the single decker, had a number of advantages: for one thing, the driver couldn't shut the door if the bus was full, so if the conductor wasn't looking, or wasn't forceful enough, passengers just kept piling on - and it was great fun riding along on the platform, hanging onto the pole and watch-ing the road rush past. Then, you could jump on and off between stops - though you sometimes got an earful from the conductor or conductress for doing so - and you had a choice between the lower deck, where smok-ing was banned as of 7th July, 1941, and the upper deck where smoking was still permit-ted. Schoolchildren tended to prefer going upstairs because the top-deck travellers were on the whole more tolerant of noise than the rather more genteel passengers downstairs. Also, it gave you a cast-iron excuse if your parents happened to notice that your hair smelt of cigarette smoke when you got home.

Above: Accrington's bus service began in the late 1920s. Prior to that the town had had electric trams, and prior to those, steam trams; in fact, trams of one kind or another trundled up and down the streets of Accrington for almost half a century. The Accrington Corporation Steam Tramways Company Limited was formed in 1885, and its steam trams, affectionately known as the Baltic Fleet, started running in 1886. Electric trams took over in 1907, and for a quarter of a century the red-and-cream electric trams were a vital part of Accrington life; it was once calculated that by the end of March 1928 the fleet had travelled over 14,000,000 miles and carried in excess of 168,000,000 passengers. There were both single-decker trams and double-deckers, as was later the case with buses; double-deckers could not be used on certain routes because of low bridges. By the early 30s the new omnibuses had succeeded in winning the vote of towns and cities all over the country. Accrington began to phase its trams out, and by 1932 the last tramroute route - along Burnley Road - had closed. Now we look at pictures of trams with great nostalgia, and it has to be said that this particular bus, while no doubt very good at its job, is rather lacking in elegance. However, among the people who

Above: The arrangements for buses in Peel Street - where they should stand, which direction they should travel in, how much space should be allocated to them - have been the subject of much discussion over the years, and much activity as well. A newspaper report in January 1938 provides the solution to a matter which must have puzzled many people: the sudden appearance of some interesting new white markings on Market Ground. Apparently proposals for a new bus station were under consideration, so the markings on the ground had had been put there to indicate the proposed layout; this, the article explained, would help the General Purposes Committee to imagine a bus station and ornamental gardens on the site. Moving on to the next decade, more bus station plans were being drawn up after the end of the second world war, and the next design seems to have received approval around 1950, although it was not until 1963 that work on that arrangement actually began. More rethinks have followed, and whether or not the present arrangement will last very far into the 21st century remains to be seen.

Left: Not the result of something going off the rails, but part of a major bridge remodelling project in 1936. As can be seen, the original bridge which carried the railway over Nuttall Street was a narrow, arched structure with limited headroom - no doubt perfectly adequate for the road users of 1846, but rather less well suited to road haulage in the 1930s. Indeed, getting large loads into the Willows Lane area by road became a tricky business. So steps were taken to make Nuttall Street a viable route for high vehicles: the bridge was widened and the arch was squared off to provide more headroom, thus creating the more functional, if less characterful, Nuttall Street bridge which most readers will probably remember. When this line was closed in December 1969 the bridge became redundant, the deck was taken away, and soon all traces of the structure will have disappeared. So before Nuttall Street bridge passes completely out of sight and out of mind, we will briefly retell the tale that has been handed down from generation to generation concerning a particular stone in the bridge, which has unfortunately vanished, although pictures of it remain. On it were carved two letters and a little matchstick-like figure. Apparently, when the bridge was under construction in 1846 the corpse of a young girl, a murder victim, was found hidden amongst the bridgeworks; and it was her initials which one of the stonemasons on the site chose to carve on the stone, out of sympathy, as an unofficial memorial to the poor girl.

Above: PC John Curson and PC Matthew Walling became Accrington's first motorbike cops in the summer of '29. The primary function of motor patrol constables, as they were known, seems to have been basically the same as that of any other police constable - to patrol their beat; the advantage was, of course, that they could travel much greater distances on their motorbikes than could a PC Plod on foot or a bobby on a bicycle, and so cover the outlying parts of the borough. The man on the right with the Norton is PC Walling, and the man on the left is PC Curson; the bikes were Messrs Curson and Walling's own, and they each received a maintenance allowance to cover their expenses, originally set at 5/- per week but doubled later in the year.

In addition they were issued with the special blue britches and leggings seen here. It is to be hoped that they were also provided with gauntlets and some means of keeping their ears warm in winter; motorcycle helmets were of course not compulsory in 1929. On the subject of police headgear, how many readers know that during the first decade of the 20th century Accrington's police force was once issued with wide-brimmed felt hats? These made the policemen look rather like cowboys, especially if worn at a jaunty angle, but unfortunately the hats were not well suited to our Lancashire climate; it was found that they became extremely heavy and unpleasant to wear when soaking wet, and the boys in blue soon went back to their cork helmets.

Above right: The posters on the coach and the somewhat grim smiles are enough to tell us that they are intent on business, not pleasure. This delegation from north-east Lancashire's hard-pressed cotton industry - representing Accrington, Barrowford, Brierfield, Burnley, Nelson, Padiham and Rishton - is heading for the capital to draw attention to the problems being faced by the industry.

It is a struggle which had been going on for many, many years by the 1950s, when these delegates were immortalised by the camera. After serious troubles in the late 1920s matters had come to a head in July 1929 when cotton workers were locked out; the following month they reluctantly accepted a cut in wages. Another major crisis came in February 1931, when a delegation from our area went to London to oppose eight-loom weaving; again they were forced to compromise and eventually they did accept more looms per weaver. Matters did not improve after the war, and foreign imports and new synthetic materials combined to bring the cotton industry to its wits' end. In August 1958, 500 people converged on Accrington Town Hall to protest at the government's failure to step in and help the cotton industry; 3,000 jobs had been lost the previous year, and the future looked bleak. Finally the government did take action, and in doing so effectively implemented a drastic pruning of the industry by making substantial compensation available to mill-owners who went out of business, thus tempting more and more mills to close. By 1962 just 18 cotton mills were left.

Below: Accrington's grocers are traditionally a lively lot, taking an active interest in local trading conditions and debating pertinent issues such as Sunday opening (which incidentally the Local Grocers' Association voted against in 1930). Their diary of events included monthly meetings, regular outings to places of professional interest such as canning factories, and social occasions as well; the occasion pictured here falls into the latter category, as we are informed that this is a Grocers' Picnic to Southport. No hampers are visible, but we trust they were somewhere on board, stuffed full of tasty morsels. The coach apparently considers 20 miles per hour the speed to aim for, and the average speed would most likely have been significantly below this, so according to our calculations it would have taken them a good hour and a half to get to Southport. The grocers would certainly have been ready for a nice warm cup of tea when they arrived! Though it may seem slow to us today, at that time an average of 20 miles an hour over a journey of a reasonable length was the most anybody should expect. This, at least, was the view expressed in 1928 by a motoring publication called The Light Car & Cyclecar. It did add, however, that an experienced motorist driving a sports car could hope to average 30 miles per hour.

Bottom: They're plainly off for an excursion - destination unknown, although the year is probably around 1925 or earlier. We are informed that this very fine coach, a Palladium, belonged to Mr Parker of Parker & Morland and was garaged at Lodge Bank near the Star Works, Antley. This ingenious contraption was a dual-purpose vehicle: the passenger-carrying body could be removed and our coach then became a lorry, and was in fact used as a coal wagon - though you would never guess it, from its immaculate appearance. Lorries which could be converted into char-a-bancs were popular with firms all over the country, as they could be used as

normal delivery vehicles during the week and converted into leisure transport at the weekend - a real bonus! The party seen here seems to be enjoying fine weather for its excursion, but the coach does have a hood, which can just be seen folded down at the back. Putting the hood up would keep the rain out, but not the cold, and it is hard to imagine that the vehicle's heating system was very sophisticated, so it is not surprising to see all the passengers are togged up in coats and hats. Looking at the cobbled road surface and the rather solid-looking tyres one wonders, too, how advanced the suspension was, although this was not such a problem as speeds were unlikely to exceed 20 miles per hour - which is a good thing, as otherwise some those hats would never have stayed on!

Shopping spree

Below: This parade of shops used to be known as Piccadilly. It stood just opposite the Town Hall, between Dutton Street and St James's Street; on the St James's Street corner, not visible on this photograph, was a piano shop. One of the first objectives which Accrington's town planners set themselves in the 20th century was the widening of Blackburn Road. They began at the other end, demolishing properties along the south side towards the viaduct and taking the building line further back. Piccadilly's turn came in the late 1920s; this picture was taken in 1926, and its death sentence has already been pronounced. The businesses appear to be doing their best to carry on as usual, but with large signs advertising the spot as a very valuable building site to be sold by auction on Monday 17th May 1926, it is clear that their days are numbered. After their demolition, Burton's was among those who took advantage of this central site, and indeed if you go round the corner into St James's Street today and look up, you will still see the inscription Burtons Chambers on the stonework, written in the distinctive curly lettering that was the firm's trademark. Montague Burton established a branch in virtually every town and city in Britain, and their good quality menswear has remained popular through the generations. The story goes that when soldiers were demobbed they used to go along to Montague Burton's with their clothing vouchers to get fitted out with civvies, and that is where the expression 'the full Monty' comes from, though these days it has come to mean something rather different from a full suit of clothes!

Accrington's Woolworth's was built in 1924 on the corner of Blackburn Road and Dutton Street; the site was formerly occupied by a row of two-storey shops which included E. J. Riley's and McRae's watchmakers and jewellers, but they were knocked down so that Blackburn Road could be widened. The familiar gold lettering on the red background soon became a magnet for shoppers, and generations have grown up knowing that whatever you need, the chances are you'll find it at Woolies. Woolworths first came to the UK with the tag of the '3d and 6d Stores', a translation of the original American '5 and 10 cent Stores'. The original '5 and 10 cent Stores' had spread across America towards the end of the 19th century, ever since F W Woolworth had had the brainwave of

setting up in business to sell a wide range of goods at fixed low prices, opening his first stores in 1879. It proved a magic formula; by 1911 he had a chain of over 1,000 shops in the USA, and he and his brother C S Woolworth subsequently expanded into the UK, Canada and Europe. All over Britain, Woolies became an institution - not only for shoppers, but for the many schoolgirls whose first taste of working life was as a Saturday girl, perhaps standing behind the sweets counter, and for the permanent employees who have never had to worry about job security. Other shops have come and gone, but Woolworth's has always been there (well, not always on this particular corner, but they haven't moved far) and we hope they stay with us far into the future.

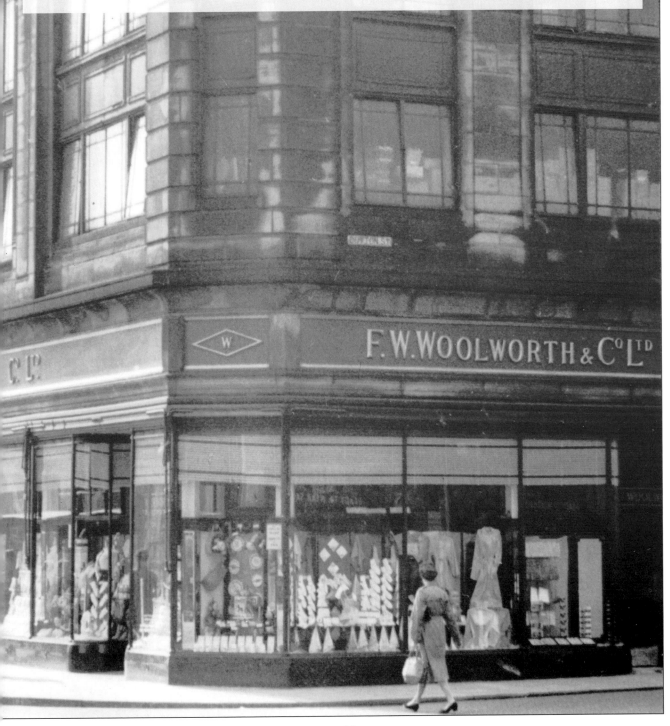

Bottom: Peel Street is seen here in another era - one in which the Maypole Dairy need have no qualms about sitting right next door to a ladies' outfitters and a gentlemen's tailor and advertising butter, cream and dairy products. And why should it? As a nation we did not, by and large, sink into a deep depression if the tape-measure revealed an extra quarter-inch on the hips, back in the 1920s; nor did we count our calories, nor worry our heads about saturated fats and cholesterol. R G Kidd's clientele had even less need to watch their figure, as men's trousers were invariable held up by braces and were accommodating enough to provide a reasonable amount of leeway around the waistline. Many older men never adopted trousers with waistbands when they were introduced in the 1950s, as they found braces much more comfortable. So much for men's attire; for the ladies, fur coats were fashionable, and Foster's could advertise furs without the slightest risk of tempting animal rights activists to stock up on eggs at the Maypole, to lob at Foster's windows. Wasn't life simple? Well, not when rationing came along in the next decade, and ration coupons seemed to get you less and less every week. However, Maypole Dairy was there to help housewives through the war; and then, when redevelopment began to change the face of town centre shopping, it relocated to Broadway, and in fact notched up the distinction of being the first of the new shops to open there, on 22nd August, 1961.

Right: The Electricity Showrooms were built at the junction of Burnley Road and Whalley Road at a cost of £4,325 including the initial site clearance, and opened on 10th March 1927. During their first two years' trading their turnover topped £14,000, and certainly one of their window displays seems to be attracting great attention - what was the big attraction, we wonder? Electrical gadgets had begun to make life easier for the housewife in the early years of the 20th century, particularly the early twin-tub electric washing machines which revolutionised wash-day. By the second world war most homes had electricity, but do you remember the plethora of different sockets and plugs that we had to cope with? Small items could run off those little 5-amp plugs with round pins, while power-hungry appliances like kettles and fires needed big 15-amp plugs, with bigger round pins; so your home had some 5-amp sockets and some 15-amp sockets. You couldn't run a 15-amp appliance from a 5-amp socket, but sometimes you wanted to plug a 5-amp plug into a 15-amp socket, so you needed a special adapter; and when 13-amp plugs with square pins appeared on the scene you needed even more adapters so you could fit square pins into round sockets as well as little pins into big sockets. By the 1970s the 13-amp plug had become standard, so when people next had their homes rewired they were finally able to throw all their adapters away with a sigh of relief, and life became that much simpler.

pushing a pram - have you noticed that babies don't howl their heads off in the open market nearly as much as they do in supermarkets? - perhaps even at that young age they find the open-air atmosphere more relaxing. And further along still, two smartly-dressed young men seem to be checking out the talent. Of course, we have allowed ourselves a little poetic licence in interpreting this little scene - but a market certainly fires the imagination more than a bus station does.

Top: A quintessential view of mid-20th century Accrington, with its famous 21-span viaduct visible in the background, the Market Hall looking impressive if a little dirty, and the market in full swing. For centuries Accrington has been a market town at heart, and will remain so, we trust, for many more centuries to come. The outside market has been shuffled around a fair bit over the years, but it doesn't matter too much where the market is, just so long as our favourite stalls are still there, together with that wonderful market atmosphere that has brought generations of shoppers from the surrounding area along with their shopping bags every week, come rain or shine. Note the mother in the foreground who appears to be teaching her child the magic formula: look right, left, and right again, and if all clear, quick march! The wonderful pram towards the right of the picture is worth mentioning too - although today's modern buggies have the advantages of being adjustable, light and easy to fold up, the capacious baby carriages of the 50s and 60s, with their solid coachwork, were very handy for stowing your parcels in alongside baby!

Above: Say Peel Street, and two things spring to mind - markets and buses. Peel Street has been torn between the two ever since buses first came to Accrington in the late 20s, and even before that it served as the official tram terminus. Its position, running along the side of the Market Hall, makes it ideally suited to both functions, since bus passengers are also likely to be market shoppers, so they want to be able to get on and off the bus close to the market. On this photograph from the late 1950s, the market has pride of place - although it just so happens that there is a bus in the picture too - and we have a fine tableau of people doing all the things that make market shopping so enjoyable. The lady setting off across the crossing from right to left armed with two large bags looks intent on doing some serious shopping, while the group crossing from left to right is already laden with parcels. On the corner a young lad is keeping himself amused by using the railing as a climbing frame while his mother chats to an old acquaintance. Further along another mother is

Broadway is a-bustle with pedestrians on this very 60s-looking snapshot, suggesting that pedestrianisation was already overdue. The co-existence of the umbrella market and the Odeon fix the date somewhere between 1962 and 1967, as after 1967 the cinema was renamed the Classic. However, most people who remember it at all remember it as the Odeon; it was opened in 1937 as the Regal, but became part of the Odeon chain eight years later and kept this name for some 30 years. No doubt many of our readers will have been among the 1,800 children who joined the Odeon Club after the second world war and went along every Saturday morning to enjoy a preliminary sing-along (conducted by that irresistible little ball which crossed the screen bouncing from one word to the next) followed by a good

THE POUND IN YOUR POCKET

In the 1920s and 30s meals were still being produced on the old kitchen range. Only the better-off could afford a gas cooker; in 1928 you would have to pay around £25 for the new appliance - around 17 weeks' wages.

Mars bars sold for 2d when they were first produced in 1932. Mars became the UK's best selling chocolate bar - and by the end of the 20th century (by that time costing 30 pence) around three million were eaten every day.

Wages were rising in the 1930s - but slowly. Two million were still unemployed. In 1939 rump steak cost 1/6d per lb, while pork sausages were 6d. Food, clothing and petrol rationing was introduced in 1940, allowing a weekly ration of a shilling's worth of meat.

Far fewer people spent their money on DIY in the 1930s and 40s. Wallpaper had to be trimmed with a pair of scissors, and paste was made with flour and water. Brilliant white paint - unknown before then - began to transform our homes in the mid 50s.

picture show - and all for sixpence. Post-war Accrington, along with the rest of the nation, began to watch more and more television, and fewer people bothered to go to the pictures when they could switch the box on and stay in their own armchair. By the end of 1967 the cinema had changed hands again and become the Classic; another owner converted it to a multi-screen cinema in 1973, and the 'super cinema' of the thirties finally came to the end of its allotted span in March 1990, when it was closed to allow the site to be redeveloped once more.

At work

Below: Question: How many men does it take to lay a couple of metal setts? Answer, according to this photograph: ten - one to pour the concrete, two to position the setts, one to hold a broom and six to watch! This experimental road surface was put down in Abbey Street in December 1931, using setts manufactured by Howard & Bullough. To the safety-conscious 21st century motorist, the idea seems distinctly odd; of course one can quite see that the metal setts would provide a very hardwearing road surface, and were cheaper than granite setts, but surely they would be slippery in the wet? We should remember though that traffic speeds in the 30s were significantly lower than they are today, and also that relatively little research had been done into the effects of tyres and road surfaces on roadholding. Incredible though it seems, up until the late 1960s there was no legislation on the minimum tread permissible on tyres; before that you could drive around quite legally on tyres bald as coots. It is only during the last 50 years or so that the efforts of independent bodies such as the Transport and Road Research Laboratories, in co-operation with car manufacturers, have raised public awareness of road safety factors, and highway engineers are still working on improved anti-skid surfaces, road markings which retain their visibility in the wet, and so on. Some ideas work, some don't; this particular experiment clearly seemed worth trying to the civil engineers of the day. It will be noted, however, that Abbey Street today has a conventional tarmac surface, from which we can deduce that it was not a success.

Right: A touch of the exotic in the middle of early 20th-century Accrington: on market days, this Italian lady used to take up her position at the kerb on the Peel Street side of the market, and many a tired and fractious child must have been cheered by the promise of a balloon or a flag. Of course, the lady must have seemed fascinating in herself, simply because she was Italian. Some 50 years before cheap flights and package holidays shrank the world to a more manageable size, Europe was an awfully long way away and only the adventurous ones among us went abroad for their holidays at all. Going abroad meant, as often as not, going to London and catching the boat train for France. Few ordinary folk had been as far as Italy. Nor were we accustomed to seeing European-style food on the menu or on sale at the supermarket. These days pizza and pasta are so familiar to us that we scarcely think of them as foreign, but even the recipe for spaghetti bolognese - now a great boon to many an inexperienced young host giving their first dinner party - would have been unfamiliar to the passers-by captured on this snapshot. In 1920, if a thing wasn't British, then it was foreign and therefore strange and exciting. And just to add to the Italian balloon-vendor's cosmopolitan mystique, she apparently had a pair of love birds which used to help her read fortunes, though quite how they did this is not clear.

This fine array of bicycles was captured by the camera in Accrington Market in 1905. Cycling had caught on in a big way by this time - though if you haven't tried it yet, the man will give you lessons. As well as being fun, a bicycle offered a practical means of independent transport, and many people, both gentlemen and ladies, became real enthusiasts. Indeed, the hobby was so universally popular that there were regular cycling columns in the newspapers alongside the motoring columns; the cycling column in the Accrington Observer, written under the pseudonym of Roadster (who was he?), gave details of runs organised by the local clubs along with general information, comments and opinions on the various aspects of cycling. The cycle business was definitely a growth area. Rather than simply buying and selling pre-assembled cycles, many dealers would buy components from various manufacturers and build the cycles themselves, selling them under their own brand name; there is a sign here advertising Quinton Cycles - Specially Built To Order. This stall seems to have something to suit all tastes - who could resist a Road Racer for £12 0s 0d, guaranteed? Cycling does not seem to have been cheap, though; a good secondhand Dunlop tyre for £3 10s 0d, when brought into line with inflation, is surely much more than we would pay for a part-worn tyre today. Note the ladies' cycles with netting fitted to the rear mudguard to cover the top part of the back wheel, so that their skirts did not get caught in the spokes.

Above: We are informed that this local family ran a successful business in the Ranger Street area during the 1920s, selling bleaching fluid in the summer (presumably to keep the outside privvies smelling nice and clean in the hot weather) and blackpeas in winter. Although it looks like a sunny day on our picture, we assume that blackpeas are in the pot today, as the young gentleman appears to be about to consume a spoonful from his mug. Peripatetic vendors are a part of life which has quietly disappeared over the last 50 years or so, and now only the ice-cream man is a common sight. At one time hawkers came round with handcarts, and later with vans, selling all manner of things including vegetables, fish and bread - and then there was the rag and bone man with his horse and cart who came round collecting your scrap; so you could stock up on groceries and earn yourself a few pennies without ever stirring far from your own front gate. You knew exactly when to expect the breadman, and the fishman, and the vegetable man, and you had your coppers ready and planned your meals accordingly. And while you queued up to be served you would chat to the neighbours and keep up with the latest gossip. It all helped create that spirit of neighbourliness which many people are nostalgic for - though fortunately there's more neighbourliness left in Accrington than in many towns and cities around the country.

> *At one time hawkers came round with handcarts, and later with vans*

Help and understanding when it is needed the most

The family business, the Wolstenholme Funeral Service has been providing a caring and confidential service to the people of Accrington since the year 1935. It was in this year that Frank Wolstenholme made the decision to expand his business to include a funeral service. Previously, Frank had spent his time working for himself as a cabinet maker and joiner. In this vein, he had built up a valuable wealth of experience and expertise and so, decided to take these skills and channel them into a different line of work.

Wolstenholme Funeral Service

We serve any time day or night

Willows Lane, Accrington BB5 0RT TEL. 232604 (24hrs)

We serve the whole of Hyndburn

Therefore, in 1935, the Wolstenholme Funeral Service was established. Frank began work in his new business using the same premises he had worked from as a joiner and cabinet maker. These premises were situated at 42 Abbey Street in Accrington. Initially, all the coffins were made individually in the workshop from solid oak or English elm. At the time, Frank only owned one machine that could be used in the construction of the coffins. The machine in question was a circular saw run by a petrol driven motor and all other work had to be done by hand, including the French Polishing!

In the early stages of the business, the main line of work was embalming which was carried out for other funeral firms. These firms covered a radius of over 30 miles from Accrington, stretching to Manchester, Rochdale, Skipton, the Rossendale Valley, and the Ribble Valley. However, as the other funeral firms became more specialised, they trained their own staff in this area of expertise and did this work for themselves. Indeed, the main line of work also changed for the Wolstenholme Funeral Service to reflect its expansion and development.

Frank's burgeoning business soon began to flourish and it was not long before his son, Raymond Wolstenholme was able to join his father making Wolstenholme Funeral Service a family business.

Above: *A compliments slip.* ***Right:*** *The exterior of the Wolstenholme Funeral Service, showing the private road.*

As soon as Raymond left school he started working alongside his father. Indeed, it was under Frank's careful guidance and training that Raymond managed to qualify through the British Institute of Embalmers in the year 1958.

Sadly, five years later in 1963, 28 years after founding his business, Frank Wolstenholme died. However, it was then that his son, Raymond, after having gathered valuable experience and expertise under his father, was able to take over the running of the family firm. Indeed, Raymond remains the present day owner of the company today, as well as its Managing Director.

In the early days of the funeral business, like most other firms at the time, the Wolstenholme's hired funeral vehicles from a central carriage master. There were two central carriage masters in the area; J W Lord in Bridge Street Church and Taylor Brothers Taxis situated at the junction of Broadway at the bottom of Whalley Road, Accrington. However, in the year 1967, the company had become successful enough to be able to introduce its first funeral fleet of vehicles.

A year later, in 1968, the Wolstenholme Funeral Service developed further. It was in this year that the firm obtained land in Willows Lane in Accrington, on the former site of St Peter's School. This land was elevated and as such, was perfect for the new funeral home as it could not be overlooked

into the funeral vehicles before driving into the main flow of traffic. The landscaped gardens also gave families a feeling of openness and peace of mind. Indeed, these well planned funeral facilities have now been appreciated by the people of Accrington for over 30 years.

Today, the Wolstenholme Funeral Service is continuing to provide help, understanding and a caring service to local families when they need it the most. Indeed, as the firm continues into its seventh decade it is set to see the third generation of Wolstenholme's joining the family business. Kelvin Wolstenholme, the grandson of the founder, has also trained and qualified through the National Association of Funeral Directors and the British Institute of Embalmers and, no doubt, will carry the family business on in its caring tradition for many years to come.

Top: The dignity of a horse drawn hearse.
Above left: The operation still runs smoothly, even during adverse weather conditions. Below: Just one of the fleet of luxury limousines.

and so retained a private atmosphere. Since taking over the business, Raymond had taken on and trained many newcomers and indeed, was a great advocate of introducing women into the business in order to maintain a sensible balance of staff. By the end of the 1960s, Raymond's expertise in the industry was recognised and as a consequence, he became Chairman of the local branch of the National Association of Funeral Directors.

The decade of the 1970s opened with an important event for the firm. In 1970, the first purpose built funeral home in the district was built comprising: a Chapel of Rest; an office; a garage; and private parking facilities. The site also had a private road which offered mourners the opportunity to assemble

The company dressed to impress

The Accrington based company, Simon Jersey Group Limited was originally founded in 1971. Throughout its existence the company, which now operates as a leading designer and supplier of uniforms and corporate clothing to business and industry world-wide, has remained true to its Lancashire roots and is still based in the town of Accrington.

It was at the beginning of the 1970s, following a period in ladies fashion retailing, with ten shops in the North West area, that Simon F Moyle summoned his entrepreneurial spirit and made the decision to set up his own uniform manufacturing company. Consequently, Simon Jersey Limited came into existence. The new business was set up from humble beginnings. At first, Simon could only afford to rent premises. These premises, which consisted of a tiny office below a tap dancing school, could not because of their location, have been

Above: *Simon Moyle, President of Simon Jersey.*
Right: *First uniform produced for The Walton Arms pub/restaurant, Altham, by the company in the early 1970s.* ***Below:*** *Staff outside the first company premises in Church Street in 1987.*

the most serene of working environments! However, with the help of the three employees that Simon hired, the business soon found its own rhythm. With an annual turnover of £20000 for the first year of its existence Simon Jersey Limited had taken its first steps on its now, well trodden path of consistent growth and development.

The following ten years from 1971 to 1981 were filled with a constant stream of work. The majority of this work came in the form of small orders from hotels and restaurants and it was these orders that enabled the business to develop steadily, gradually building up a reputation for reliability and quality. As a result, at the end of the first ten years of the company's life, in 1981, the annual turnover had increased to £97,000 and Simon Jersey Limited now employed four people. It was also in this year that the company's first catalogue was produced.

The years in the latter half of the 1980s proved to be eventful ones, bringing the first extensive changes to the company as well as a period of rapid

development. In 1985, Simon Jersey engaged its first distributor in Norway and three years later the company was able to move out of its original small offices to a larger, custom built building. In 1989 a corporate division of the company was started to run alongside the catalogue, offering bespoke ranges for larger businesses and institutions.

The 1990s opened with yet another mark of success for Simon Jersey Limited. It was in 1990 that, due to the increase in sales and number of employees, the company moved once again, this time to a specially designed 6,000 square metre building in the same business park. Indeed, the decade continued as it had started. In 1992 the company was able to enter the French market and by 1993 Simon Jersey products were being distributed in 23 overseas countries. The year 1994 was distinguished with a visit from HRH The Princess Royal to company headquarters and a year later the company achieved yet another distinguished success - the certification to ISO 9001.

In 1996, the company's Silver Jubilee year, Simon Jersey Limited celebrated 25 successful years of growth and proceeded with an extension to its headquarters to accommodate further development. Indeed, this development was quick to follow and only a year later the company could boast four versions of its catalogue in five languages produced to fulfil the clothing requirements of all sectors of business and industry world-wide. As well as completing another extension to the company's headquarters in 1998, making it up to 10,000 square metres, this year also saw Simon Jersey receiving several awards in the

categories of Design, Customer Service, Marketing, Export and Business Acumen. These awards were added to a year later with a RIBA Architectural award for the design of the company's headquarters in Accrington.

Today, Simon Jersey Limited employs 300 people, has an annual turnover in excess of £26 million and sells more than 2.3 million garments a year to over 110 countries! With over 1,000 ready-to-wear styles and an 'A la Carte' menu of designs made to individual order, there is no doubt that Simon Jersey Limited will continue to perform as a company 'dressed for success' in Accrington for many more years to come!

*Top left: An image from the company's first brochure from 1982. **Top right:** Simon Moyle (left) with David Trippier (then MP Rossendale). **Above right:** Clothing from the Simon Jersey catalogue 2000. **Right:** Simon Jersey Headquarters at Altham Business Park.*

Home and away - a story of success

ew professional people would risk financial suicide by launching into business in a declining field. Yet Steve Thompson and Catherine Wolfenden were so confident that their innovative ideas would bring success that this is exactly what they did. Britain was in the middle of a recession, with the property market languishing in the doldrums, when in a management buy-out from their former employers the partners committed themselves to the founding of a new estate agency in Blackburn Road, Accrington.

Their total commitment to the venture, however, paid off - and at the heart of their success lay the unique package they offered their clients. The scheme involved a combination of different incentives which could be offered to purchasers in packages which could be tailor made to suit, including subsidised mortgages, free legal fees, free accident, sickness and unemployment cover, refund of survey fees and payment of stamp duty. The exclusive mix-and-match incentives were a hit with clients, who proved keen to take advantage of the scheme which was worth anything from £500 to £2,000.

The scheme was only one of the innovative ideas which Steve Thompson and Catherine Wolfenden had up their sleeves. Many of their rivals had so many properties on their books that they were unable to advertise them all - a major criticism among frustrated house owners anxious to sell up and move into a new home. Recognising the importance of regular advertising, the partners adopted the policy of advertising clients' property in the local press every couple of weeks, while at the same time, every house on their register was displayed in the office.

Few estate agencies recognised the advantages of renting properties. Mr Thompson, however, argued that when people were contemplating a move to a different town, perhaps at the other end of the country, they didn't want to spend hours on the motorway before searching, often unsuccessfully, for a suitable property. Renting a house in their chosen area would give them a base to work from and the leisure to search for exactly the right new home. Prospective buyers could spend time in the locality, not only looking at houses but also at the availability of good schools for their children, nearby shopping centres, good roads and convenient public transport. The scheme had a second benefit; clients who had had difficulty in selling empty houses were given the option of renting the property for a while, then putting it back on the market again at some later date.

Eighteen months after the launch of the business in 1992 the partners were able to open a second

Below: The Accrington premises.

branch, conveniently situated in the centre of Great Harwood. Financial advisor John Ruggieri then became a partner in this branch and together with his colleague Jamie McFarlane entered the business at this point; they would be free to see clients at either of the offices or, if it was more convenient, would be willing to visit clients in their own homes.

Both Steve Thompson and Catherine Wolfenden are fellows of the National Association of Estate Agents - the only country-wide representation of professional estate agents. Chairman of the North West branch since 1992, Mr Thompson was subsequently elected President of the north west branch of the organisation. The connection with the NAEA gave the partnership the advantage of being the only estate agents in Hyndburn who had access to Homelink, a register of estate agents around the UK, the Channel Islands and Europe. Their association with the NAEA made it possible for them to link clients with a reputable estate agency in the area they hoped to move to, whether it was Bradford or Bruges.

Further expansion followed hot on the heels of the opening of the Great Harwood branch. In 1995 the champagne corks popped again as yet another branch of Thompson &

Partners was set up, this time in Bank Street, Rawtenstall and David Stubbs joined the firm as the fourth partner. The partnership was going from strength to strength, and once again, expansion was the proof of success. In all the offices, personal attention by the partners remained at the top of the priority list, and clients could rest assured in the fact that the people they were dealing with were all well qualified in their own field of expertise. Thompson & Partners were the first estate agency in East Lancashire to qualify for ISO 9000 accreditation - a real feather in the cap that crowned their achievements over the years.

And what of the future? Well, more of the same, certainly: personal service, innovation which includes adopting more new technology - and most of all, the same dedication to excellence which brought runaway success to the partnership.

Thompson & Partners face a bright future as they enter the new millennium.

*Top left: The office at Great Harwood. **Below:** A row of cottages bearing Thompson & Partners 'sold' and 'for sale' signs in Rawtenstall.*

Delivering three generations of family achievement

The year 1893 was to prove to be an important one in the history of the Accrington company, Hoyle and Dean Limited. It was in this year that George Hoyle was born and indeed, 30 years after his birth, in 1923, George founded Hoyle and Dean Limited.

Before founding his own business, George had spent his time wisely. He started his working life productively, working for Lang Bridge, an engineering company based in Accrington. It was whilst working for them that George witnessed the advent of the first world war. As a consequence of the outbreak of war George temporarily left Lang Bridge in order to join the Royal Flying Corps and serve his country.

After the cessation of the war George returned to Accrington. It was in the town, in 1920, that George met and married Emily Jefferson. However, this was not George's only successful union. At around the same time, George met his brother-in-law, Tom Dean. This meeting was to prove to be another vital event in the history of Hoyle and Dean Limited. George's ambitions stretched beyond his work at Lang Bridge and he was determined to establish his own company. Indeed, in 1923 this is just what he did. With the financial help of Tom Dean, George managed to purchase his first lorry and the haulage business, later to be known as Hoyle and Dean Limited, was born.

George started the burgeoning business at premises in Hollins Lane. Ironically, when he collected his first lorry and brought it to the garage facilities at Hollins Lane, Tom could not even drive! George's wife, Emily played a significant role in the new business. She worked from home, where the Hoyle's had one of the first telephones in Accrington, and did the firm's books.

With Emily's help, George's business soon began to flourish. In 1931, George and Emily's son Harry, who was to play a significant role within the business in later years, was born. Only six years after this happy event the business experienced its own success. It was in 1937 that George was able to expand the business and move to larger premises at Water Street and Gilles Street from which they began trading as a haulage contractor and a car repairer.

By 1945, Hoyle and Dean had progressed enough to be in a position to be able to join the Road Haulage

Top left: Company founder, George Hoyle.
Below: Harry standing alongside one of the first of the new vehicles in the early 1970s.

Association. Two years later, in 1947, Harry Hoyle began working for George's brother, Uncle Harry Hoyle at Wilkinson Tools, Warrington. This is where he met his future wife Joan. However, in the year 1950, Harry made the decision to follow in his father's footsteps and consequently, he joined Hoyle and Dean.

Harry's progress within the business was temporarily halted when in 1952 he had to serve his National Service R E M E. However, when he returned in 1954, Harry soon resumed his successful habits, helping his father to ensure the continued success of Hoyle and Dean. The year 1955 was a landmark year for the business. It was in this year that Hoyle and Dean became a Limited Company with George, Emily and Harry Hoyle acting as the Company's first Directors.

In 1961, the Company had become successful enough to be able to hire its first Transport Manager, Jack Duckworth. Indeed, a year later with Uncle Harry's financial assistance, Hoyle and Dean Limited purchased new premises at The Drill Hall in Argyle Street, Accrington. After the completion of extensive alteration work, the business moved to these premises and Frank Hartley was employed to run the General Office. In 1965 John Scott joined the Company to run the Mechanics Workshop and after investing in the business he was also made a Director. Indeed, two years later the Company was able to open an office in London.

In 1973 the founders grandson, David, joined the family Company and began work as a lorry driver. David's mother, Joan, and Frank Hartley became

Directors in 1974 and Alan Dearden was employed as the new Transport Manager. Sadly, in 1975, the Company's founder, George Hoyle, died. However, in the same year another of his grandson's, Michael, joined the Company ensuring its continuation as a family concern. Indeed, only five years later, in 1980, David and Michael became Company Directors. David started work in the Traffic office, Michael eventually transferred to the General Office and their mother, Joan, became Company Secretary.

Sadly, in 1985, Harry Hoyle died. However, the third generation of Hoyles carried the Hoyle name forward. Indeed today, with the help of the Company's many loyal and long serving staff, the founder's grandchildren are still ensuring that Hoyle and Dean Limited remains a successful concern and that it maintains the personal, specialised service that has earned it a very loyal customer base.

In 1998 to celebrate 75 years the 2nd, 3rd and possibly the 4th Generations celebrated with a Hog Roast Barbecue together with customers, suppliers and friends past and present.

*Top left: One of the company vehicles taking part in the Accrington Carnival. **Above left:** Harry Hoyle wearing the Transport Managers Club medallian. **Above right:** Present day staff and vehicles. **Below:** The 2nd, 3rd and 4th generations celebrating at the 75th anniversary Hog Roast Barbecue in 1998.*

Providing a training ground for success

I t was during a meeting on the 28th August, 1969 that the decision was taken to form what is now known as the North Lancashire Training Group. The Training Group was to be funded by the Furniture and Timber Training Board and set up under the name, North East Lancs Training Group. Indeed the Group, consisting of 12 member companies, held its first meeting in the October of that year at Cannon Street in Accrington and agreed on the mission statement, 'to improve efficiency and productivity by better training methods'.

By the May of 1970 the Group had appointed its first Group Training Officer, John Allsopp. Three months later, a room at 15 Cannon Street, Accrington was leased at a rent of £3-0s-0d per week and it was from there, in the November, that the Group held its first AGM.

With the new Group fully established, work to meet the company's mission statement could now begin. Indeed, in 1971 the first course run by NLTG was held on Budgetary Control and Forecasting and attended by 17 people. In 1972 John Allsopp left the group and was replaced by Jim Harkness, the present managing director.

In 1973, with a view to increasing the number of applications from school leavers, the Group decided to visit every pertinent Careers Office and promote their services. It was also in this year that Maths, IQ and Mechanical Ability tests were introduced for all applicants.

In 1974, it was announced that Training Groups would only receive government funding up until July 1975. In light of this decision the members of the NLTG agreed that they would financially support the Group in order to ensure its continuation and that a Think Tank, concentrating on the extension of the Group's activities would be established. This was accomplished and consequently, in 1975, The North East Lancs Training Group absorbed the North West Group and its staff. The amalgamated Group was renamed, the North Lancs Training Group and larger premises at Arndale House, Accrington were leased. At that time, the Group had £10.44 in its bank balance and a total of 22 members and a staff of three. However, this was soon to change as the Group's workload was about to dramatically increase!

By 1976, the Group was almost entirely self funded. 1977 saw visits to exhibitions and factories in Italy and Germany and the implementation of new courses including a Health and Safety course and an Outward Bound course for the 12 best apprentices. In 1978 the Group purchased their first of what now amounts to £100,000 worth of films.

This was followed, a year later, by the production of the first NLTG Training Times news letter, the purchase of 85 Whalley Road and the introduction of a vocational training pilot scheme.

Above: *Mr and Mrs Fernando of Leksha Industries Ltd, Sri Lanka, on a fact-finding visit in 1984, with a view to setting up a furniture components factory.*
Top: *The Tramway, Accrington, purchased by the North Lancashire Training Group for conversion to office premises in 1984.*

On the 10th January, 1981 Margaret Thatcher announced that all Training Boards were to be scrapped. Indeed, by 1982 this had happened and as a result, nationally, only five of the 54 Training Groups survived! The NLTG was one of the survivors and carried on its invaluable work, introducing a Youth Training Scheme for the Manpower Services Commission. Indeed, by 1984 the Group was able to purchase the Tramway Public House for conversion into offices and in 1985 the Group became a Limited Company with a Board of Directors.

By the time the Group celebrated its 20th anniversary, in 1989, it had introduced more courses and a Fork Lift Truck Training School. The 1990s opened with the signing of contracts with eight Training and Enterprise Councils, the purchase of its first three company cars, and the opening of an office in Cumbria. By 1994 the Group had purchased further premises, become the first company in the North West to achieve an Investors In People Award, taken over training for the furniture industry in Northern Ireland, obtained a BSS 750 Quality Award and,

reached a turnover of £1 million for the first time! 1995 was a year of firsts for the Group. Not only was the first Effective Management course started in Northern Ireland but, the first NLTG Snooker Competition was held raising £2,000 for the local Scanner Appeal and, premises in Infant Street were purchased giving the Group its first shop window base in the town. A year later Jim Harkness was invited, along with 12 other managing directors and chairmen to have a meeting with the Duke of Edinburgh to suggest ways of financially supporting the Outward Bound organisation. As a result NLTG and other companies agreed to support the organisation to the tune of £10,000 a year for five years. Consequently, the Group's letterheads were redesigned to incorporate the patron's emblem.

By the group's 30th year, in 1999, two Sewing Machining Training Centres had been opened in Blackburn and Rochdale, two further premises had been purchased, and the Group could boast that 99 per cent of its apprentices and trainees went on to be employed. Some 12,000 youngsters having now been on it's training programme.

Today, the North Lancashire Training Group continues to flourish, as do its trainees. The Group now employs 65 staff, owns 35 company cars, runs over 480 courses, and has over 1750 trainees. Indeed, with the help of its 80 Member Companies, the Group will, no doubt, continue to provide a training ground for success for the people of Lancashire, the north west of England and Northern Ireland for many years to come.

Far left: The Infant Street Premises which were officially opened in June 1996. Left: The new Information Technology Training Centre in Dutton Street which opened in September 1998. Below: The Accrington based team.

Keeping pace with Old Father Time!

The year 1987 was an important one in the history of Accrington town as it was in this year that the Arndale Centre opened. However, it was as far back as 1935 that Accrington Corporation first discussed the possibility of some form of central shopping facility for the town. It was in this year that Blackburn Road was linked to Burnley Road by a new road named, Broadway. This £28000 new road provided a thoroughfare around which a new commercial centre could be developed. Indeed, the construction of Broadway paved the way for the whole of Accrington's central area shopping strategy over the next 50 years!

The advent of the second world war meant that any plans for a central shopping area were put on hold. It was not until the end of the 1950s that the building of town centre complexes took off throughout the country and Accrington, anxious not to be left behind, planned its own scheme. A new block of shops were to be built along one side of Broadway on the former site of the Union Buildings Mill and the Wesleyan Methodist Chapel and School. A new outdoor market was planned as was a new central bus terminus.

In 1961, the new shopping block was opened under the name, Arndale House. The name 'Arndale' actually originates from the names of Arnold Hagenbach and Sam Chippendale, who set up Arndale Property Trust Limited, one of the first development companies in the country to build shopping centres. The new scheme was indeed, developed by Arndale Property Trust Limited, which became Town and City Properties Limited in 1968 and later, Sterling Guarantee Trust Plc. The scheme cost £500000 and the fact that Marks and Spencer opened its first store since the war at Arndale House, also played a significant part in the centre's immediate success.

A decade later, in 1971, it was realised that Accrington was losing trade to local town shopping centres in Blackburn and Burnley. As a result, a Shopping Subject Plan was carried out which found that Accrington was the most important convenience shopping centre in the local area and that retail development was essential for a successful future. It was not until 1978 that the decision was made to develop a large council owned car park at the rear of the Marks and Spencer store into a shopping centre and it was hoped that the new site would be opened by 1982.

Unfortunately, this initial timetable proved to be a little optimistic. The council had chosen a firm, London and Manchester Securities, to develop the

Above: The sunken gardens on Broadway pictured during the 1950s. They were bulldozed soon after to provide the site for the new Arndale block.
Below: Broadway pictured in 1960 as work began on the first phase of the central area redevelopment scheme, the Arndale shopping block.

centre. All seemed to be going well until there was a disagreement between the two parties over the council's insistence that car parking should remain free. With no prospect of a compromise, the project was scrapped and it was then that Sterling Guarantee Trust Plc took control of the scheme, enabling the plans to become, at long last, a reality.

In 1983 it was decided that the covered shopping centres, managed by Sterling Guarantee Trust Plc, required a special sort of management and so, Arndale Shopping Centres Limited was set up to provide this new function. In 1985, the company merged with P&O and it was in this same year, at a press conference/public meeting that the plans for the Accrington Arndale Centre were revealed. A model and drawings on display at the meeting showed that the centre was: to be built with the tough, red Accrington bricks; have an L-shaped, glass-roofed, pedestrian mall; a 600-space multi-storey car park; 29 shops under cover; and a design to harmonise it with Arndale House. Sally Hopkinson, a Graphic Designer was to design the interior of the centre incorporating a Victorian theme with colour codes and fruit symbols. The £7 million development was to be funded with £5 million of the developers money and with a government Urban Development Grant of £177,500.

By 1987 the centre was complete and in a topping out ceremony, two bay leaves were placed under the final coping stone which, according to folklore, would ward off evil spirits. The actual opening ceremony began when the centre's new ornamental clock, sculpted by Andy Plant, burst into song at midday on 29th October. The clock, in the shape of the world with a sleeping Old Father Time on the top

joined by a school boy and several cherubs, began to spin on the hour and opened to reveal a fun band playing 'Rock Around the Clock'! The opening ceremony was performed by the Mayor, Bill Parkinson who was assisted by comedian, Ken Dodd and was followed by three days of street enter-tainment for the people of the town.

Indeed, the Accrington Arndale Centre proved to be a great success for the town. It provided Accrington with the right amount of new shopping floorspace needed in order to regenerate town's retail industry as well as providing over 110 new jobs for the town. Today, the centre continues to thrive and has, in fact, become a vital part of the heritage and identity of Accrington's retail industry.

Above: New building work underway in the mid 1980s. *Below:* Comedian, Ken Dodd, officially opens the new Arndale Centre in October 1987.

The opening of the Young
People's Library in June 1938

Acknowledgments

The publishers would like to thank

Lancashire County Council Accrington Local Studies Library for permission to reproduce photographs from their extensive collection. We also acknowledge the assistance given by the staff at the Local Studies Library in Accrington, in particular Helen Barrett and Catherine Duckworth.

Howard Talbot of Howard Talbot Photography in Blackburn who kindly loaned several sports and 'press' photographs, taken either by himself or his late father, Wally Talbot.

John Goddard who kindly edited the book.

*Thanks are also due to
Margaret Wakefield who penned the editorial text and
Ann Ramsdale for her copywriting skills*